JUST REVENGE

JUST REVENGE

COSTS AND CONSEQUENCES
OF THE DEATH PENALTY

MARK COSTANZO, PH.D.

ST. MARTIN'S PRESS
NEW YORK

Design by Maureen Troy

Library of Congress Cataloging-in-Publication Data

Costanzo, Mark.
    Just revenge : costs and consequences of the death penalty / Mark
Costanzo.
        p. cm.
    ISBN 0-312-15559-X
    1. Capital punishment—United States. I. Title.
HV8699.U5C67   1997
364.66'0973—dc21   97-17045
                                                                CIP

First edition: November 1997

10 9 8 7 6 5 4 3

For my father,
who disagrees with me about the death penalty
and most other issues

Let us call it by the name which, for lack of any other nobility, will at least give the nobility of truth, and let us recognize it for what it is essentially: a revenge.

—Albert Camus

But though vengeance be the motive, it is not the purpose of the death penalty. Doing justice and deterring crime are the purposes.

—Ernest van den Haag

Acknowledgments

I've heard that some people can write a book in their spare time. I'm not one of those talented, disciplined people. So, first I would like to thank my primary employer, Claremont McKenna College, for granting me a nine-month sabbatical from my teaching duties. Second, I am grateful for the generous support of the John Randolph Haynes and Dora Haynes Foundation. Many of the ideas and findings presented in this book grew out of my research on the death penalty. That research investigated jury decision-making and attorney arguments in capital murder trials. The Haynes Foundation financed my research and later provided a summer grant that enabled me to begin work on this book.

Writing a book is a solitary pursuit. Because most of the work is done sitting alone in front of a computer screen, it's often hard to know what you've neglected and what you've failed to make clear. Fortunately, good reviewers can point out weak arguments, neglected evidence, and poorly written passages. Several of the most prominent death-penalty scholars in the country generously agreed to read and comment on one or more chapters of this book. Reviewers included David Baldus, Hugo Bedau, William Bowers, Sally Costanzo, Steve Davis, Richard Dieter, Mike Farrell, Robert Johnson, Richard Moran, David Myers, Diann Rust-Tierney, Gerald Uelmen, Margaret Vandiver, and Franklin Zimring. This book is much stronger because of their efforts, and I am grateful for their help. Of course, I am to blame for any deficiencies that remain.

I would also like to thank the people at St. Martin's Press. My initial editor was Sheila Cavanagh. Sheila was the first to see the promise of this book. Although she has since left St. Martin's, I am grateful for her help. I am especially grateful to Gregory Cohn, my current editor. Greg read every word in this book several times and made wide-ranging comments on clarity, style, structure, and content. His insight, enthusiasm, and editorial skill have improved the book dramatically. Greg not only continues to serve as my editor, he doubles as a knowledgeable guide to the peculiar and mysterious world of trade book publishing.

Finally, I thank my family. I first became interested in the death penalty when my wife and I were dating. Sally was working as an investigator for death-penalty cases. Her job took her to dangerous places and required that she meet with unsavory people. Concerned about her safety, I often went along for the ride. That was my introduction to the inner workings of the death penalty. Not only did Sally get me interested in this topic, she read and commented on every chapter of this book. I am deeply grateful for both her perceptive comments and her constant support. Our daughter, Marina, also deserves thanks. For her, this book was an immense drain on her father's time. It meant less playing, less biking, and fewer trips to the beach. She was gracious beyond her years.

Contents

JUST REVENGE

Introduction

The death penalty has found new life in the 1990s.

- In 1992 Robert Alton Harris was killed in a California gas chamber. His was the first execution in California in a quarter century.
- To remove all doubt about his support for the death penalty, candidate Bill Clinton interrupted his 1992 presidential campaign and flew back to Arkansas to preside over two executions.
- In 1993 Wesley Allen Dodd was hanged by the state of Washington, the first person to be executed in that state in twenty-nine years.
- In 1994, the crime bill passed by Congress expanded the use of the death penalty to over fifty new federal crimes (including such crimes as the murder of a poultry inspector), and Kansas responded to public outrage over violent crime by restoring the death penalty. By the end of 1994, Maryland had carried out its first execution in thirty-three years, Nebraska had killed its first prisoner in thirty-five years, and Idaho had resumed executions after a thirty-six-year hiatus.
- In 1995, New York's newly elected governor fulfilled a campaign promise by restoring capital punishment, making New York the thirty-eighth state to authorize executions. During 1995, fifty-six people were executed, the highest yearly total since 1960.
- In 1996, a new federal law limited death-row inmates to a single federal appeal unless new evidence provides "clear and convincing" proof of innocence. By the end of 1996, Oregon had carried out its first execution in thirty-four years.
- In 1997, Arkansas executed three prisoners in a single night.

As we move through the final years of the twentieth century and enter the new millennium, the already hot topic of capital

2 | JUST REVENGE

punishment is likely to get much hotter. There are now over 3,200 condemned prisoners on death row—more than at any time in U.S. history.* Fear of violent crime is at a near-record high, and politicians continue to clamor for more executions. Now is the time for a critical analysis of the costs, benefits, and consequences of the death penalty. This book is an attempt to provide such an analysis. Drawing on research evidence accumulated over several decades, I will argue that it is time to abandon the death penalty.

---

*Because more that 98 percent of the prisoners on death row are male, masculine pronouns are used throughout this book when referring to capital defendants or condemned prisoners.

CHAPTER ONE

A Long Bloody Past

Then shall his father and mother lay hold on him, and bring him
unto the elders . . . and say this our son is stubborn and rebellious,
he will not obey our voice; he is a glutton and a drunkard. And
all the men of his city shall stone him with stones, that he die. So
shalt thou put evil away from among you; and all Israel shall hear,
and fear.
                                                          —*Old Testament*

Those who shew no mercy should find none; and if hanging will
not restrain them, hanging them in chains, and starving them, or
. . . breaking them at the wheel, or whipping them to death . . .
should.
                    —*Paper presented before the English Parliament (1701)*

Before there were prisons there was the penalty of death. In
ancient times, executions were usually accomplished by stoning. These brutal events were often little more than spontaneous
eruptions of mob violence. Stoning remained the dominant form
of execution for hundreds of years, and gradually the practice
became, if not more civilized, at least more ritualized and formal.
Among the ancient Greeks and Hebrews a clear etiquette of execution emerged. All that was necessary to trigger a stoning was
an accusation by two witnesses with good standing in the community. Accusers would place their hands on the head of the
defendant and describe the crime they had witnessed. The
doomed man or woman was then walked, carried, or dragged to
a tall rock or an elevated scaffold. With hands tied, the convict
was stripped naked and then pushed from the platform by one of
the witnesses. The second witness had the honor of casting the
first stone. If the condemned man still showed signs of life, the

people gathered to watch the execution joined in until the victim's bloody body lay motionless beneath a pile of rocks.[1]

Many other forms of killing were soon devised. "Death by a thousand cuts"—where small bits of flesh were carved away over a period of days—was sometimes used in ancient China. During the rule of the Rajahs in nineteenth-century India, elephants were sometimes used to make executions especially excruciating:

> The culprit, bound hand and foot, is fastened by a long cord, passed round his waist, to the elephant's hind leg. The latter is urged into a rapid trot through the streets of the city, and every step gives the cord a violent jerk, which makes the body of the condemned wretch bound on the pavement. . . . Then his head is placed upon a stone, and the elephant executioner crushes it beneath his enormous foot.[2]

In England, from as early as 1241 to as late as 1820, those convicted of capital crimes were hanged, drawn, and quartered. The prisoner was taken from his prison cell and laid on a sledge, which was tied to a horse and dragged along the ground to the gallows. At the gallows, the prisoner slowly strangled while dangling from a rope (the "long drop," which snaps the spinal cord, was a modern innovation in hanging). The executioner was often instructed to cut down the prisoner when "half dead," at which point the convict was disemboweled, his entrails thrown into a nearby fire, his head cut off, and his body cut into quarters.[3] The decapitation and "quartering" of the transgressor served both dramatic and practical ends: It added power to the execution ceremony and provided five parts of the corpse that could be displayed at conspicuous sites as visible warnings to potential wrongdoers. Indeed, during the seventeenth and eighteenth centuries, many major crossroads in London were decorated with decaying corpses hanging from trees or stuck on poles. London Bridge was adorned with the heads of the recently executed, such heads having been "parboiled" (cooked in salt and cumin seed) to delay the decaying process and render them unappetizing to birds. Judging from an account in 1665, this process was apparently quite effective:

> And here I cannot omit to declare unto you the miraculous sight of this head, which, after it had stood up the space of fourteen dayes upon the bridge, could not be perceived to waste nor consume; . . . but grew daily fresher and fresher, so that in his lifetime he never looked so well; for his cheeks being beautified with a comely red, the face looked as though it had beholden the people passing by, and would have spoken to them. . . . [4]

Stoning and hanging were not the only methods of execution in early times—only the most common. An impressive amount of sadistic creativity went into devising methods of killing those who dared to break the law. Some techniques involved little preparation or equipment: throwing the offender into a quagmire to drown; beating to death with fists, feet, and sticks; and beheading by sword or ax. More elaborate forms of execution included "breaking on the wheel" (popular in eighteenth-century Germany and France) and "pressing to death."[5] The "wheel" involved binding the hands and feet of the criminal to a large cart wheel. The wheel was positioned on an incline with the criminal facing outward to afford a better view of the spectacle. It was important for the audience to have a clear view because public officials believed that witnessing these gruesome executions would inspire fear and keep others from breaking the law. The executioner, wielding an iron bar, methodically broke the arms and legs in several places before bringing death by a blow to the throat or the heart. The procedure might involve as many as forty blows and last as long as two hours.

"Pressing" took longer and was generally reserved for those

who were reluctant to confess to crimes they may or may not have committed. The prisoner was stripped naked and tied, face-up, to the floor of the prison cell while iron or stone weights were loaded on him. More weights were piled on each day, producing agony but not death. The execution procedure required that the prisoner "shall have no more sustenance but the worst bread and water," and that "he shall not eat the same day on which he drinks, nor drink the same day on which he eats; and he shall so continue until he dies."[6] Not surprisingly, this procedure was almost always successful in extracting the desired confession.

For more than a century capital punishment was not confined to humans. In several European countries, animals who killed humans might also find their way to the gallows. Of course, pigs, cows, and horses could not provide useful testimony on their own behalf, but humans could provide eyewitness or character testimony. Attorneys defended animals accused of murder in trials quite similar to those afforded human defendants. In 1396 a pig accused of fatally injuring a child was dressed in the suit of a man and publicly hanged.[7] In 1750 a man and a donkey accused of having sexual intercourse were scheduled to be burned together at the stake. In the end, the donkey was spared because a local priest and other leading citizens testified that the beast was of noble character and an unwilling participant in the depravity. The man, however, was not so lucky.

Method and style of execution depended not only on the gravity of the crime but also on the gender and social standing of the offender. Burning at the stake was typically reserved for women. Though burning is surely a hideous way to die, it was considered far less excruciating than the disemboweling and quartering that men faced for similar crimes. A woman who was tarred and bound before the fire was lit could be "mercifully" strangled at the stake before the flames enveloped her body. There was also the question of decorum. As Sir William Blackstone explained, women were granted the more dignified method of death because "the decency due to their sex forbids exposing and publicly mangling their bodies."[8] Blackstone adds that such small kindnesses reveal the "humanity of the English nation." In England, one final accommodation was made to women: pregnancy could postpone or prevent execution. If the condemned was known to be or suspected of being pregnant, a panel of twelve matrons was appointed to investigate the matter further. If the panel determined that the prisoner was with child, a stay was granted. But mercy had its limits—many women were hanged shortly after giving birth in their prison cell. In 1931, a law was passed forbidding the death sentence for pregnant women.

Executions in the United States

Nearly four centuries have passed since the first documented lawful execution on American soil in 1608 (Captain George Kendall was killed for the crime of theft in Virginia).[9] Although early colonial laws were adapted from British law, capital punishment in the colonies was both more humane and more restricted than in seventeenth-century England. At a time when drawing and quartering, disemboweling, and burning at the stake were still commonplace in the civilized countries of Europe, hanging—at the time regarded as the most humane method—was almost always the means of execution in the colonies. However, just as in Europe, hangings were festive public spectacles. The condemned was forced to take a slow wagon ride to the gallows, often sitting atop the very coffin he or she would soon occupy. The rowdy crowds who witnessed the hangings often numbered in the thousands.

Under British law at the time, there were more than fifty capital offenses (including vagrancy, heresy, witchcraft, rape, murder, and treason)[10] while, on average, only about a dozen crimes were punishable by death in the colonies. But lists of capital crimes varied widely by territory. Puritan-influenced Massachusetts Bay Colony listed statutory rape, rebellion, adultery, buggery, idolatry, witchcraft, bestiality, man-stealing, and blasphemy as capital crimes. In contrast, Quaker-influenced South Jersey declined to adopt capital punishment in its original charter. Behaviors that threatened property or the social-economic order were often designated as capital crimes. In North Carolina, for example, capital offenses included circulating seditious literature among slaves, inciting slaves to insurrection, slave stealing, and harboring slaves for the purpose of setting them free. Similarly, Virginia listed only five capital crimes for whites, but seventy for blacks![11]

Lynching, an unofficial form of execution, was widespread in early America. Those who were frustrated with the workings of the legal system often formed spontaneous mobs of vigilantes. Although records are sparse, it appears that the number of lynchings peaked during the 1890s, when 1,540 were performed. This exceeded the number of state-authorized executions by 442.[12]

The Abolition Movement

The movement to abolish the death penalty in America has been marked by a long series of advances and retreats. In 1787, at the home of Benjamin Franklin, influential citizens of Philadelphia gathered to hear an eloquent speech by Benjamin Rush, a physician and signer of the Declaration of Independence. Rush, whose thinking was indebted to the Italian Enlightenment thinker and jurist Cesare Beccaria, argued that executions brutalized the population and were an improper use of state power. Rush's efforts gave momentum to the abolition movement, and by 1793, Pennsylvania's attorney general, William Bradford, proposed the notion of *degrees* of murder. Bradford defined first-degree murder as "willful, deliberate, and premeditated killing" or murder committed during "arson, rape, robbery, or burglary." His distinction was formally adopted the following year, and use of the death penalty became restricted to first-degree murder. Pennsylvania also launched a national trend in 1834 by banning public executions. Although public executions were quite rare after the dawn of the twentieth century, public interest in such spectacles had not waned. In 1936, this country's last public hanging (in Kentucky) attracted a crowd of nearly twenty thousand.[13]

In 1838 Tennessee abandoned mandatory death sentences for capital crimes and gave jurors the option of imposing a sentence other than death. A few states went even farther. Michigan eliminated capital punishment for all crimes except treason in 1846, twenty years earlier than any European nation. Rhode Island and Wisconsin became the first two states to eliminate capital punishment for all crimes in 1852 and 1853, respectively.[14] At least until the early 1900s, the abolitionist movement appeared to be gathering momentum. But most states that experimented with abolition later reinstated the death penalty (e.g., Colorado, Kansas, Maine, New Mexico, and Oregon). At present, thirty-eight states and the federal government have laws authorizing capital punishment. States without the death penalty include Alaska, Hawaii, Iowa, Maine, Massachusetts, Michigan, Minnesota, North Dakota, Rhode Island, Vermont, West Virginia, and Wisconsin.

Of course, there is a difference between laws authorizing capital punishment and actual executions. Throughout U.S. history, the number of death sentences and executions has always been small when compared with the number of murders. Individuals convicted of murder are rarely executed. The rate of execution peaked in 1938, when there were 2.01 executions per 100 homicides in states with the death penalty. Even for capital homicides—the murders the legal system considers the most abhorrent—the execution rate is less than 10 percent.[15] The annual number of executions was highest during the 1930s and reached a record high in 1935 when 199 people were put to death. Following the 1930s, the number of executions declined steadily for 27 years until they halted for nearly a decade. Between June 3,

1967, and January 17, 1977, no one was executed in the United States. This moratorium was aided by low levels of public support for capital punishment, and there was presumably little political will to carry out executions when the future of capital punishment was in doubt.

In 1972 the Supreme Court evaluated the constitutionality of the death penalty in the case of *Furman v. Georgia*. Evidence of "arbitrary and discriminatory" sentencing persuaded the Court that the death penalty, as then administered, violated the Eighth Amendment's prohibition against "cruel and unusual punishment." In *Gregg v. Georgia* (1976) and its companion cases, however, the Court decided that, by restructuring the capital trial and guiding the discretion of jurors, death sentences could be applied fairly.[16] The moratorium on executions ended in 1977 when convicted murderer Gary Gilmore halted further appeals on his behalf and demanded to be executed by a Utah firing squad. Since Gilmore's execution, nearly 400 people have been executed. More than three-quarters of these executions have taken place in five southern states: Florida, Georgia, Louisiana, Texas, and Virginia.

Why We Must Kill the Killers

In ancient times, one murder would often incite several other murders and provoke an expanding "blood feud." A victim's family might seek vengeance by killing a member of the murderer's family, provoking a long cycle of murder and retaliation. By seizing control over the punishment of murderers, the state preserved community order and restricted the scope of killing. A murder was avenged by taking only the life of the murderer, and the nearest relative of the victim was sometimes permitted to serve as judge and executioner. This method of satisfying the urge for revenge maintained social order and prevented blood feuds from spinning out of control.

Capital punishment was not the only penalty for murder. For

example, the Anglo-Saxons developed an elaborate system of fines. Instead of killing the murderer, a payment to the family of the victim could sometimes be substituted, with the assessed fine depending on the official value of the victim's life: "If a freeman slew his thrall, he paied a nominal fine to the king for a breach of the peace; but if a slave killed his master the doctrine of blood for blood was carried into effect."[17]

Early justifications for killing wrongdoers rested on religious authority. Religious leaders insisted that executions were a means of carrying out the will of God. According to the laws of Moses, the death penalty was a way to appease God and avert famines, plagues, and other misfortunes that might result from "God's fierce anger" against any community that failed to punish sinners. The sinner was killed in order to "purge the evil from the midst of you."[18] In New England, the religious nature of the execution was made explicit by the practice of having ministers deliver a sermon from the gallows as a prelude to a hanging. These sermons, which were delivered routinely from 1674 to as late as 1825, relied heavily upon Scripture and emphasized the community's duty to avenge God and avoid his wrath. Spectators were warned that "if we will not pronounce such a villain accursed, we must be content to bear the curse ourselves. . . . The land cannot be cleansed, until it hath spued out this unclean beast."[19] As American society became more secular, scriptural justifications began to lose some of their resonance. Simple vengeance then rose to become the dominant justification. Vengeance served as a compelling justification for several decades, until religious and political leaders began to challenge the morality of revenge.

Justifications for the death penalty rested not only on divine law but also on human order. Noah Hobart, a leading Connecticut minister, argued in 1768 that the goal of punishment was social peace and security and that the seriousness of a crime is measured by the "tendency to destroy the public good, or the safety and happiness of society."[20] The moral authority of the state was highlighted by emphasizing the fairness of the legal procedures that led to conviction and execution. By 1800 gallows sermons reminded audiences that the condemned prisoner "had the assistance of the most able counsellors and advocates, who appeared to adduce every argument and motive that might possibly operate in your favar."[21] Further, the prisoner was reminded that "the evidence was so clear against you as to induce twelve sober, judicious, disinterested jurors, on their oath to pronounce you guilty."[22]

Deterrence, with its considerable commonsense appeal, has always been the most prominent feature of arguments seeking to justify capital punishment based on its social benefits. According to the deterrence argument, the death penalty actually saves lives by discouraging potential murderers. The Greek philosopher Pythagoras expressed faith in the principle of deterrence, and the Roman philosopher Seneca argued that "the more public the punishments are, the greater the effect they will produce upon the reformation of others."[23] English thinkers such as William Paley helped shape the American colonists' view of the utility of punishment. In 1790, Paley wrote that the aim of punishment was not revenge but "prevention against future offenses of the same kind . . . by deterring others by the dread of his example."[24] The theory of deterrence remains a major justification even today.

Leaving aside the validity of the theory of deterrence for the moment (it is the subject of Chapter 6), its ascendance poses a fundamental problem: If punishment deters, then harsh punishments should deter best, and the very best results should be obtained if many types of crimes are punished in the harshest possible manner. If the penalty of death deters murder, then it should also deter theft or adultery or blasphemy. And if the possibility of death isn't a powerful enough deterrent, death could be made more terrifying by torturing before execution and mutilating the corpse after death. As noted by one historian, "No means was deemed too foul, too savage, or too inhuman, if it were thought to prove an effective deterrent."[25] Today, while justifications based on divine law and deterrence persist, their relative importance has faded. Other rationales for support or opposition have moved to the foreground: financial cost, fairness of application, revenge, discrimination, wrongful conviction, and public support. These issues are closely examined in the chapters that follow.

Historical Trends

The death penalty has evolved over many centuries. If we look carefully at this long evolution we can spot four consistent trends. The first trend has been a dramatic shrinking in the number and types of crimes punishable by death. For some 150 years in England (until the death of George III in 1820), more than 200 crimes were punishable by death. Petty theft and other crimes that seem trivial by modern standards could cost a criminal his or her life. As one observer put it, "We hanged for everything—for a shilling—for five shillings—for witchcraft—for things that were and things that could not be."[26] In most countries the list of capital crimes kept getting shorter until the death penalty itself was finally erased from the law of the land. The renowned attorney Anthony Amsterdam sees this trend as "the slow but absolutely certain progress of maturing civilizations that will bring an inevitable end to punishment by death."[27] In many countries this "inevitable end" has already been reached. The United States now stands alone as the only Western democracy that still executes its citizens.

Even in the United States, lists of capital crimes have been steadily shortened so that, in most states, they now include only first-degree murder with "special circumstances." Circumstances that define a murder as "death eligible" vary from state to state but generally include the following: (1) murder committed in the commission of a felony (e.g., robbery, rape, or kidnapping);

(2) multiple murder; (3) murder of a police or correctional officer acting in the line of duty; (4) especially cruel or heinous murder; (5) murder for financial gain; (6) murder by an offender having a prior conviction for a violent crime; and (7) causing or directing another to commit murder. Approximately 80 percent of capital cases involve defendants charged with the first circumstance, murder during the commission of a felony (so-called felony-murder).[28]

A second trend involves the attempt to lessen the cruelty of executions by replacing one execution technology with another, seemingly more humane, technology. Without exception, the claim has been made that each new method was quicker and less painful than its predecessor. For example, Dr. Guillotin confidently declared that the victims of his killing device would feel nothing more than a "slight sensation of coldness on the neck." In a similar vein, Ronald Reagan used a folksy analogy to suggest that lethal injection might produce a quick, painless death for condemned prisoners:

> I know what it's like to try to eliminate an injured horse by shooting him. Now you call the veterinarian and he gives it a shot and the horse goes to sleep—that's it. I myself have wondered . . . if there aren't even more humane methods now—the simple shot or tranquillizer.[29]

In the 1800s hanging was the most common means of execution. It was eventually replaced by electrocution, then by lethal gas, and, most recently, by lethal injection. Currently, 27 states use lethal injection, 11 use electrocution, 4 use lethal gas, 2 use hanging, and 1 uses a firing squad. In states that authorize more than one method, the condemned prisoner is usually able to choose the means by which he will die.

Although each change in the method of killing was designed to make executions more humane, questions have been raised about the "humaneness" of every method. The question of whether execution is cruel and humane is central to the death penalty debate and will be examined at length in Chapter 3.

A third trend has been the attempt by policy-makers to ensure that death sentences are imposed fairly and rationally. To make imposition of the death penalty fairer, courts and legislatures have, at various times, enacted mandatory death sentences for specified crimes, forbidden the practice of mandatory death sentences, broadened the sentencing discretion of jurors, and narrowed the sentencing discretion of jurors. Unfortunately, these efforts have failed to produce a fair and rational system of capital punishment. This issue of fairness will be discussed in Chapter 5. Race, social class, and even geography continue to influence which defendants are sentenced to live out their lives in prison and which are sentenced to die in the execution chamber.

The fourth trend involves what might be called the sanitizing of executions. In the 1700s and early 1800s, executions were usually public events witnessed by hundreds or thousands of rowdy spectators. A carnival atmosphere prevailed, and the day's festivities often included several hangings. Execution was swift, often occurring only days or weeks after conviction. In contrast, today's executions are conducted late at night, using well-defined and specialized procedures. These modern events are witnessed by only a handful of observers (e.g., journalists, relatives of the condemned prisoner, relatives of the victim) and occur, on average, eight years and five months after conviction.[30] Unfortunately, the well-intentioned regulation of our system of capital punishment (and even the use of such euphemisms as "capital punishment") has the secondary effect of enabling citizens to distance themselves psychologically from the act of killing. Albert Camus made the point forcefully nearly forty years ago:

The survival of such a primitive rite has been made possible only by the thoughtlessness or ignorance of the public. . . .

When the imagination sleeps, words are emptied of their meaning: a deaf population absent-mindedly registers the condemnation of a man. But if people are shown the machine, made to touch the wood and steel and to hear the sound of a head falling, then public imagination, suddenly awakened, will repudiate both the vocabulary and the penalty.[31]

In our time, the public imagination still sleeps, but it is an uneasy, fitful sleep. As prisoners pile up on expanding death rows, the crushing costs and troubling consequences of the death penalty become much harder to ignore. This book is an attempt not only to "show the machine," but also to expose the social, political, moral, and economic consequences of killing people who have killed.

CHAPTER TWO

From Trial to Execution Chamber

If you want to vote for death you each have to ask yourself: Could I be the one to drop the cyanide pill? Could I do that? Sentence him to gag to death in a green room?

—Defense attorney in capital murder trial

I don't think anyone would vote for the death penalty if they had to do it—you have to judge this person, you have to say this guy has to die.

—Juror in capital murder trial

I magine that you are a juror. You have just convicted a man of first-degree murder with special circumstances. You and eleven other jurors must now decide whether this man should live out his life in prison or die by execution. What information would you need to have at your disposal? What issues would you need to consider? What would convince you that someone deserves to be killed for his crimes? What might make you decide to show mercy, to send the man to a life in prison instead of the execution chamber?

How jurors decide which defendants should die has been a pivotal issue in Supreme Court rulings for more than a quarter century. Justices and legislators have tinkered with both trial procedures and jury instructions in an effort to correct problems with capital sentencing. The challenge is to fashion a process that minimizes arbitrary sentencing decisions based on legally irrelevant criteria (e.g., race, wealth, gender), while simultaneously allowing jurors to consider the unique circumstances of each case. The issue confronting the Court has been whether this delicate balance can be achieved in practice, whether death sentencing can be both fair and rational. When death is at stake, the permissible margin of error is quite slender.

Many have doubted the capacity of the courts to regulate the nature and scope of penalty decision-making. As Justice John Harlan wrote in 1971:

> To identify before the fact those characteristics of criminal homicides and their perpetrators which call for the death penalty, and to express these characteristics in language which can be fairly understood and applied by the sentencing authority, appear to be tasks which are beyond present human ability.[32]

Just prior to his retirement, Justice Blackmun came to share Justice Harlan's view. In *Callins v. Collins* (1994), Blackmun declared that his support for the death penalty had come to an end. "From this day forward, I no longer shall tinker with the machinery of death," he wrote in an eloquent dissent. After struggling for more than twenty years "to develop procedural and substantive rules that would lend more than the mere appearance of fairness to the death penalty endeavor," he reached the conclusion that our system of capital punishment still "fails to deliver the fair, consistent, and reliable sentences of death required by the constitution."

Two Landmark Decisions

Until the early 1970s, juries were given broad discretion in making the life-or-death sentencing decision. Then, in 1972, everything changed. In the landmark case *Furman v. Georgia*, the Supreme Court ruled that capital punishment—as then administered—was unconstitutional. Two constitutional questions were at issue: the Eighth Amendment's prohibition against "cruel and unusual punishment" and the Fourteenth Amendment's guarantee of "equal protection" under the law. The *Furman* decision overturned more than 600 death sentences and, because of *Furman*, a moratorium on executions that began in 1967 lasted nearly a decade.

In *Furman*, Stanford law professor Anthony Amsterdam blended legal theory with social science to wage a devastating assault on the death penalty. Amsterdam's brilliant presentation before the Court—one justice later described it as the best he had ever heard—actually consisted of four arguments.[33] First, he presented overwhelming statistical evidence that African Americans and poor defendants were far more likely to receive death sentences. Nine out of every ten people executed for rape had been black, and more than half the prisoners executed since 1930 had been black. A second argument was that the death penalty was imposed in an inconsistent and arbitrary manner; armed robbery might send a man to the electric chair while murder might lead to a thirty-year prison sentence. The death penalty resembled a lethal lottery. Third, it was argued that because the death penalty was so rarely imposed, it could not be defended as an effective deterrent to crime. From 1960 to 1964, the average number of executions was thirty-six per year. The count fell sharply after that: seven in 1965, one in 1966, two in 1967, and none at all between 1968 and 1972. The fourth and final argument was that societal standards of decency had evolved beyond the practice of killing as a form of punishment.

After hearing these compelling arguments, two of the justices, Thurgood Marshall and William Brennan, were ready to abolish the death penalty for good. Three other justices—Potter Stewart, Byron White, and William O. Douglas—joined with Brennan and Marshall to form a decisive majority. Justice Stewart concluded that the death penalty was "wantonly and freakishly applied," and Justice White observed that "there is no meaningful basis for distinguishing the few cases in which it is imposed from the many cases in which it is not." Justice Douglas pointed to "the uncontrolled discretion of judges or juries" and concluded that "no standards govern selection of the penalty." The existing system of capital punishment was ruled unconstitutional in a 5-to-4 decision.

It was a resounding victory for abolitionists, but not an enduring one. Although five of the justices had voted to strike down the death penalty, the reasoning underlying their votes differed markedly. The deeply contentious decision splintered the Court. Nine separate opinions were issued and, at more than 50,000 words, *Furman* stands as the lengthiest—and one of the most passionate—Supreme Court decisions ever. Most important, although the *Furman* majority condemned the "arbitrary and discriminatory" pattern of death sentences, it did not prohibit use of the death penalty in principle. It was merely the *current administration* of capital punishment that was prohibited.

Especially in southern states, people were angered by the *Furman* decision. Not only did the public want the death penalty restored, state legislators resented the restriction of state authority by the federal government. These legislators labored long and hard to find ways of making capital punishment constitutional again. By reworking death-penalty sentencing procedures, they hoped to ease the concerns of the Court. By 1976, the Court was ready to review several of the modified sentencing schemes. And by that time a crucial Justice, William O. Douglas, had retired and been replaced by the more conservative John Paul Stevens (appointed in 1975 by President Ford). Two of the Justices in the *Furman* majority, Potter Stewart and Byron White, seemed ready to reverse their earlier votes. The stage was set for another divisive fight over the constitutionality of the death penalty.

Two basic sentencing schemes were submitted by the states. North Carolina (*Woodson v. North Carolina*, 1976) and Louisiana (*Roberts v. Louisiana*, 1976) proposed mandatory death sentences for certain types of murder, thereby erasing all discretion. The reasoning was that arbitrariness and discrimination could be eliminatcd if there was no room for any discretion. But the facts in *Woodson* highlighted the need to take into account the unique characteristics of each case. James Woodson had waited in a getaway car while his two accomplices robbed a convenience store, killing the clerk and wounding a customer. One of the accomplices traded his testimony for a twenty-year sentence, and Woodson received an automatic death sentence for his participation. Clearly, the automatic sentencing had not corrected the inequities that led the Court to strike down capital punishment four years earlier.

Automatic death sentences were rejected by a 5-to-4 majority. The majority argued that mandatory death sentences offended the "evolving standards of decency" referred to in *Furman*, and that such laws permitted very different cases to be treated as though they were identical. According to the majority, consistent application of the penalty was essential because "the penalty of death is qualitatively different from a sentence of imprisonment, however long." The majority further explained that "[automatic death sentencing] does not fulfill *Furman*'s basic requirement by replacing arbitrary and wanton jury discretion with objective standards to guide, regularize, and make rationally reviewable the process for imposing a sentence of death."[34]

Georgia, Texas, and Florida had fashioned an alternative scheme that attempted to restrain juror discretion during the sentencing decision. This policy of "guided discretion" eased the concerns of the Court and was ultimately approved by a plurality of the justices.[35] In *Furman*, the justices had laid the blame for arbitrary application on the "unfettered discretion" afforded jurors. In *Gregg v. Georgia*, the Court approved a series of reforms intended to eliminate arbitrary and discriminatory death sentences. Under these new "guided discretion" statutes, only certain types of murder (first-degree murder with special circumstances) are eligible for the death penalty. Defendants accused of capital murder would be tried by jury in a two-phase proceeding. Guilt would be assessed in the first phase, and if the defendant was found guilty of a capital crime, sentence would be decided by the same jury in the second, "penalty" phase. In the penalty trial, the jury would answer a single profound question: Should the defendant be sentenced to life imprisonment or death by execution?

To further assure impartial application of the penalty, death verdicts would be automatically reviewed by state supreme courts. With these reforms in place, the majority was confident that the problems cited in *Furman* would be eliminated. "It seems clear . . . that the problem will be alleviated if the jury is given guidance regarding the factors about the crime and the defendant that the State, representing organized society, deems particularly relevant to the sentencing decision."[36] The majority seemed to share Justice Blackmun's belief that "the issues posed in the sentencing proceeding have a common-sense core of meaning and that criminal juries should be capable of understanding them."[37]

In its quest for fairness, the Court focused its attention on the sentencing decision-maker, which is almost always the jury. The jury is told to follow guidelines intended to restrain its discretion. Jurors must consider both the crime and the mitigating circumstances presented in the unique biography of the defendant. The new view of the Court was that guided discretion and appellate review were the key components of a constitutional death penalty.

As a result of *Gregg*, death sentences were revived. Executions resumed in 1977, when Gary Gilmore—who had halted further appeals on his behalf—was shot and killed by a Utah firing squad.

Supreme Court decisions since then have attempted to refine the penalty-phase proceedings. *Lockett v. Ohio* (1978) held that the sentencer must "not be precluded from considering, as a mitigating factor, any aspect of a defendant's character or record and any of the circumstances of the offense that the defendant proffers as a basis for a sentence less than death."[38] *Eddings v. Oklahoma* (1984) ruled that while jurors "may determine the weight to be given to relevant mitigating evidence," they "may not give it no weight by excluding such evidence from consideration."[39] *Barclay v. Florida* (1983) held that the jury may consider aggravating circumstances not mentioned in the relevant statute, and *Skipper v. South Carolina* (1986) held that evidence pertaining to the defendant's future behavior and potential adjustment to prison could be relevant sentencing considerations. In *California v. Brown* (1987) it was ruled constitutional to instruct the jury not to be influenced by "mere sympathy," and *Payne v. Tennessee* (1991) held that jurors could consider the harm that the victim's death caused his or her survivors. In general, in a series of decisions after *Gregg*, the high Court has signified that it will "no longer regulate what a penalty jury hears, except to approve the procedures by which the jury gets to hear as much as possible."[40]

How the System Works Today

Before a prisoner is killed in the execution chamber, there has been a period of confinement on death row, and there may have been a variety of appeals. Most important, there has been a capital murder trial that culminated in a guilty verdict and a sentence of death. The process begins when the defendant enters a courtroom and ends when a corpse is carried from the execution chamber. To understand our system of capital punishment, it is important to look closely at this process.

Jury Selection and Death Qualification

Potential jurors are randomly selected from a large jury pool. Prosecuting attorneys, defense attorneys, and the judge then ask potential jurors a series of questions to determine who will actually serve on the jury. This process is known as *voir dire* (French for "to see and tell"). Most potential jurors are eventually rejected. Attorneys are permitted to excuse jurors from service through "challenges for cause" or through "peremptory challenges." In a challenge for cause, an attorney will claim that a juror's answers indicate that he or she is unable to be fair and impartial or is unable to follow the law (e.g., a juror might say that she would hold it against a defendant if he chose not to testify on his own behalf). There is no limit on the number of challenges for cause. Attorneys can also oust a juror by using one of a limited number of peremptory challenges (challenges for which no reason need be stated). What is usually referred to as jury selection is actually a process of deselection: Each jury is made up of people who were not successfully challenged by either the prosecution or the defense.

The process just described is the similar to the process of assembling a jury for any other type of criminal trial. But in a capital case, *voir dire* also includes the added dimension of "death qualification." The process of death qualification is unique to capital trials. In addition to routine questions about attitudes and personal experiences thought to be pertinent to the case, prospective capital jurors are asked if they will be able to consider a death sentence if the defendant is found guilty of a capital crime. In 1985, the United States Supreme Court ruled that potential jurors whose beliefs "substantially impair" their ability to impose a death sentence should be excused from serving on a capital jury.[41] Thus, if a potential juror expresses an unwillingness to seriously consider execution as a punishment, he or she is not permitted to serve on a capital jury. From the pool of death-qualified jurors, prosecuting and defense attorneys challenge and attempt to exclude jurors whom they perceive as unsympathetic to their case.

Death qualification influences both the composition of the jury and the penalty deliberation process. The results of more than a decade of research have led to the conclusion that "juries are likely to be nudged toward believing the defendant is guilty and toward an imposition of the death sentence by the very process of undergoing death qualification."[42] The impact is both direct and incidental. First, jurors who remain in the pool after death qualification tend to be more conviction prone than potential jurors screened out by the process. They tend to be more receptive to aggravating factors and less receptive to mitigating factors presented during the penalty phase. A second, more subtle effect occurs because jurors naturally try to make sense of the odd process of death qualification. Jurors who answer a series of questions about their willingness to vote for a death sentence often conclude that both defenders and prosecutors anticipate a conviction and a death sentence.[43]

The Capital Murder Trial

The road to the execution chamber begins with the capital murder trial. The two-phase structure of the capital trial is unique in our justice system. The first "guilt" phase is similar to other types of criminal trials. Using the available evidence, prosecutors must prove beyond a reasonable doubt that the defendant committed the murder. But unlike other criminal trials, if the jury finds the defendant guilty, a second "penalty" phase begins. In this second phase jurors must decide whether the defendant should be killed in the execution chamber. Penalty phases are rare events. It is estimated that for every 100 cases in which capital crimes are alleged, only about 20 progress to the penalty phase.[44]

Jurors play a uniquely prominent role in capital trials. In most criminal cases, jurors decide only whether a defendant is guilty. Decisions about punishment, if necessary, are left to the judge, who has a better understanding of various sentencing options (e.g., incarceration, probation, diversion programs) and their availability for a given defendant. But in capital cases, these concerns are moot. The penalty phase is qualitatively different from all other types of trials because the question posed of jurors is not, What happened? but, Does this defendant deserve to be killed or spared? Conventional forms of evidence and usual standards of proof no longer apply. The judge is no more qualified than the jury to make such a profound moral choice. Indeed, the jury is believed to be better equipped; it is hoped that the jury will reflect the conscience and values of the community. Yet,

68/44

although a particular jury may provide a crude approximation of societal values, its members rarely possess experience in sentencing decisions or even clearly defined notions of who deserves the death penalty and who does not.

In the penalty phase, jurors hear testimony about "aggravating" factors (that can be used to support a sentence of death) and "mitigating" factors (that can be used to support a sentence of life imprisonment). Juries may sentence the defendant to death if aggravating factors outweigh mitigating factors. Whereas most trials focus on logic and evidence, the penalty phase focuses on the defendant's motivation, character, and life history. Moving beyond facts and evidence, defenders and prosecutors give reasons for the actions of the defendant, explore the consequences of the murder, and show how the recommended sentence is consistent with widely held moral principles. Defense attorneys must try to humanize their client by presenting a plausible explanation for the defendant's despicable behavior. If jurors are to show mercy, they must be able to see the murderer as a human being, not merely as a one-dimensional, remorseless monster whose actions are beyond understanding. This humanizing is typically accomplished by placing the defendant's violent conduct in a larger context. Brothers, sisters, parents, children, neighbors, teachers, friends, and co-workers may testify about the defendant's character and life. In a well-conducted penalty phase, the life story of the defendant is painstakingly reconstructed so that the jurors who will decide his fate can understand the events and influences that contributed to his murderous behavior.

Such testimony is not meant to excuse the defendant's violence. It is offered to create understanding, to elicit feelings of compassion, and to offer jurors reasons for voting to send the defendant to a life in prison instead of the execution chamber. One defender put it this way in his penalty-phase closing argument:

The reason I wanted you to know as much as possible about [the defendant] is that all of the factors in his life in some way determined what happened. All of us are born in this society with certain potentials, certain capacities, certain possibilities. Some of us are born into a certain family, a certain environment and all of these determine the choices we have as we grow up.[45]

Depending on the characteristics of the case, several forms of mitigation—such as mental retardation, emotional distress, abuse and neglect, mental illness, youth at the time of the crime, drug abuse, domination by others—might be presented by defenders. In addition to hearing about terrible murders described in graphic detail, jurors often hear about the disturbing world of the defendant. Many of the people who end up on trial for capital murder have grown up in a world seething with violence. Attorneys often locate the roots of violence in harrowing experiences of physical and psychological abuse. Defendants in capital murder trials have often suffered from a harsh and punishing life that includes abuse, neglect, and a lack of options. Here is an excerpt from a different closing argument describing the childhood of one defendant:

You heard about a father that beat the hell out of his mother . . . choked her unconscious, hit her so hard she had to be treated for her female organs. You heard about an alcoholic father, an alcoholic mother. You've heard about, worst of all, an overbearing, arrogant, abusive, nasty, giant brute of a grandfather. . . . Or how about the grandmother that likes to go beating up people with electric extension cords? Or how about torture? . . . Can you imagine the terror of being closed inside a burlap sack, having a rope tied to the burlap sack, having it thrown over a limb of an oak tree and having yourself hoisted. And then being smoked. . . . Can you imagine the terror of that? Does that give you a little bit of a clue of what his life must have been like? To give you a little bit of a clue why the defendant maybe doesn't see things the way we see things?[46]

The type of mitigation emphasized by the defender depends on the characteristics of the defendant and the crime. In some cases the circumstances of the crime suggest mental illness, as a different defender explained:

[The defendant] is mentally disturbed. You know it. I know it. . . . Carrying the body of your dead lover around for a couple of weeks in your apartment, lighting fires and talking to her. Sure, any normal human being does that. He's very, very sick, and he has been for a long, long time. Death is an absolute punishment. And we, at least in this country, don't kill people that are not absolutely responsible.[47]

Heavy use of alcohol or drugs is sometimes cited as a reason to assign less responsibility to the defendant:

Isn't that what alcohol and drugs do to you? They impair your ability to be a rational person, to think properly, to act right. That's why we're concerned about people who take drugs and drink in excess. And throughout the period of time when [the defendant] is involved in the planning of this, his mind is affected. His judgment is impaired by alcohol and by drugs.[48]

It is hoped that such context helps to explain the defendant's crimes and helps jurors to look beyond the crimes and see the humanity of the defendant.

Prosecutors paint a very different picture of the defendant and his crimes. If the defender's job is to humanize the defendant, the prosecutor's job is to dehumanize him. Of course, this is a far easier task given the savage nature of the defendant's crimes. In their closing arguments, prosecutors attempt to diminish, dispute, or dismiss the importance of whatever has been offered as mitigation. For example:

> He had a bad childhood, the bad childhood stuff. . . . Is that unusual? . . . Being molested as a kid is not unusual. Being beaten as a kid or hit by your dad or parents or stepfather isn't unusual, and those people don't 30 years later have the Boston Strangler come sprinting out of them.[49]

According to many prosecutors, mental disturbance is more apparent than real:

> What did the [defendants] live for? . . . For the immediate pleasures of life . . . go home sometime and look up the definition of hedonism. It wasn't because of some mental immaturity or mental problem or psychological difficulty.[50]

Prosecutors also attempt to discount the importance of mitigation by emphasizing freewill:

> He has made choices, that's what put him here, the choices he has made. Don't relieve him of responsibility for the choices he has made. . . . At every choice, at every decision making place, what has he done? He has chosen violence. As a thinking adult you take responsibility for your actions. And your actions have consequences.[51]

It is often the crimes themselves—murders so vile that they defy understanding—that provide the most powerful aggravation. Especially vicious features of the crime are recounted in vivid detail by prosecutors.

. . .

When the penalty phase begins, the defendant has already been convicted of a horrible crime, and jurors want severe and certain punishment. While prosecutors argue that death is the only fitting punishment and that jurors should "show the defendant exactly the compassion and sympathy and understanding he showed his victim," defenders argue that life in prison is sufficiently harsh punishment:

> You couldn't be lenient in this case if you wanted to be. There's no way. The law will not allow it. Personalize a little bit and think about spending the rest of your life in a six foot by eight foot room with a toilet in the middle. A room that's about the size of your family bathroom. Think about that. Living in your bathroom for the rest of your life.[52]

Attorneys also make broad philosophical and religious arguments in their final appeals to the jury. Prosecutors emphasize the legitimacy of revenge:

> [The defendant] has victimized completely innocent people. And those people deserve your attention. They deserve to be avenged. That is a very legitimate concept. I would not tell you that vengeance can be separated from what you're doing here. I would not tell you that there isn't a certain amount of anger, of retribution that is part of a decision that you make, if you decide with death.[53]

In contrast, defenders urge jurors to show mercy by linking their appeals to religious values. They implore jurors to be guided by loftier values such as compassion and by religious teachings that counsel mercy and condemn revenge:

Do to [the defendant] what God did to Cain when he slew
Abel. He banished him. Didn't kill him, he banished him.
And, that's what you will do to [the defendant]. You will
banish him forever.[54]

There is a stark contrast between the life stories told by defenders and prosecutors in the penalty phase. Defenders tell a
complex and textured story. The defendant is a tragically flawed
character, emotionally and socially deformed by years of neglect
and abuse. The origins of his violent behavior can be traced back
to early life experiences as well as powerful forces acting on him
at the time of the crime (e.g., drug addiction, domination by others, mental deficiencies, emotional upheaval). The causes of his
crimes are varied and complex. In the prosecutor's contrasting
version of the story, both plot and character are simplified. All
that is important to know about the character of the defendant is
revealed in his brutal crimes. He is an evil, remorseless monster,
motivated by little more than greed, rage, or sadism. His crimes
have little to do with any suffering in his past; they are the product of a series of free choices. The brutality of the crime and the
suffering of the victims cry out for a sentence of death.

Jurors in Capital Murder Trials

Capital jurors find themselves in an extraordinary situation.
They are plucked from their daily routines and asked to listen for
weeks or months to lawyers, witnesses, and a judge. They are
passive spectators of the courtroom proceedings, ritualistic events
that are tightly controlled by an esoteric system of rules that most
jurors cannot hope to understand fully. They hear about the grisly
details of a horrible crime, they hear the heart-wrenching testimony of those who loved the victim, and they hear about the
often barren and brutal life of the defendant. They are not allowed to talk with lawyers or witnesses or even to ask the simplest

of questions. They are expected to absorb information without participating in the search. They cannot discuss the impending decision with spouses, friends, or family members until after the decision has been made. They cannot even discuss the case with each other until official deliberations commence. In the somewhat euphemistic language of the Court, the capital jury "is made up of individuals placed in a very unfamiliar situation and called on to make a very difficult and uncomfortable choice."[55] That is, with the help of eleven other people, each capital juror must struggle to decide whether to kill another human being.

Not surprisingly, the process of making the sentencing decision is very stressful for capital jurors. Here's how a couple of jurors put it:

"I just felt a lot of pressure and I went home crying one night."

"I guess it's because you had somebody's life in your hands—it's a very big decision."[56]

"You had to argue to make the decision . . . continual arguing, tempers flared. You could see that over the days it was taking its toll."[57]

Several major sources of stress have been identified by jurors: the life-or-death consequences of their decision, hearing about a terrible crime in graphic detail, and the interpersonal strains of trying to reach a group decision during deliberation.

Jurors recognize that the sentencing decision requires a very different kind of reasoning than the logical piecing together of facts needed to determine guilt. One juror put it this way:

"Did he do the crime is much different than trying to figure out why he did it, will he do it again, what kind of person he is. Those questions are much more difficult. We relied more on gut feelings."[58]

The Sentencing-Phase Instructions

At the very heart of the system designed to channel the discretion of jurors are what the Supreme Court saw as improved sentencing instructions. These instructions are all jurors have at their disposal to structure their deliberations. But the inadequacy of such guidance is reflected in the fact that 60 percent of the death-penalty cases decided by the Rehnquist Court challenged the instructions given to capital jurors.[59]

The instructions actually list the legally relevant factors to be considered by jurors. The law tells jurors, "You shall consider, take into account, and be guided by the following factors, if they are applicable." The list of factors varies a bit from state to state, but the following list is representative.

(a) The circumstances of the crime of which the defendant was convicted in the present proceeding and the existence of any special circumstances found to be true.

(b) The presence or absence of criminal activity by the defendant which involved the use or attempted use of force or violence or the expressed or implied threat to use force or violence. Before you consider criminal activity as an aggravating circumstance, such criminal activity must be proven beyond a reasonable doubt.

(c) The presence of any prior felony conviction.

(d) Whether or not the offense was committed while the defendant was under the influence of extreme mental or emotional disturbance.

(e) Whether or not the victim was a participant in the defendant's homicidal conduct or consented to the homicidal act.

(f) Whether or not the offense was committed under circumstances which the defendant reasonably believed to be a moral justification or extenuation for his conduct.

(g) Whether or not the defendant acted under extreme duress or under the substantial domination of another person.

(h) Whether or not at the time of the offense the capacity of the defendant to appreciate the criminality of his conduct or to conform his conduct to the requirements of the law was impaired as a result of mental disease or defect or the effects of intoxication.

(i) The age of the defendant at the time of the crime.

(j) Whether or not the defendant was an accomplice to the offense and his participation in the commission of the offense was relatively minor.

(k) Any other circumstance which extenuates the gravity of the crime even though it is not a legal excuse for the crime [and any sympathetic or other aspect of the defendant's character or record] that the defendant offers as a basis for a sentence less than death, whether or not related to the offense for which he is on trial.[60]

Jurors still have considerable discretion, but far less than they had before the *Gregg* decision. The Supreme Court hung its hopes for fair death sentencing on the instructions that jurors carry with them to deliberation. The "lawless," "arbitrary," and "capricious" sentencing condemned in *Furman* would presumably be repaired through the use of clear, logical instructions. The vast and varied testimony presented during the penalty phase would be filtered through the penalty instructions, and, as far as possible, a probing moral analysis would be transformed into a systematic fact-finding mission.

At least on the surface, these "guided discretion" instructions seemed an elegant solution to the problems raised in *Furman*. But just below the orderly surface of the sentencing instructions lies a well of ambiguity. For example, when does one infer an "implied threat of violence"? What constitutes "extreme mental or emotional disturbance"? If a victim was fighting with the defendant before his or her death, does that qualify as "participation in the defendant's homicidal act"? How much duress is "extreme" and how much domination is "substantial"? There is also room for interpretation as to whether a particular factor is aggravating or mitigating. For example, if a defendant commits a murder in his early twenties, does his age increase or decrease the gravity of his crime? If the defendant was drunk at the time of the crime or if he was easily dominated by accomplices, does this make him more or less dangerous? And what if most of the factors given in the instructions are simply not applicable to a particular case? What if the defendant was physically abused over the course of his childhood? Is this a significant form of mitigation? And what if his early life was spent in a severely impoverished environment? What if his parents simply did not care for or nurture him during his formative years?

To further complicate the "guidance" given to jurors, instructions include a description of how the aggravating and mitigating factors should be combined. A weighing metaphor is to be used:

> The weighing of aggravating and mitigating circumstances does not mean the mere mechanical counting of factors on each side of an imaginary scale, or the arbitrary assignment of weights to any of them. You are free to assign whatever moral or sympathetic value you deem appropriate to each and all of the various factors you are permitted to consider. In weighing the various circumstances you simply determine under the relevant evidence which penalty is justified and appropriate by considering the totality of the aggravating with the totality of the mitigating circumstances. To return a judgment of death, each of you must be persuaded that the aggravating circumstances are so substantial in comparison with mitigating circumstances that it warrants death instead of life without parole.[61]

If, after reading the instructions, you have a clear understanding of what factors are to be considered and how those factors should be combined, you are doing better than most jurors. Jurors attempt, often unsuccessfully, to interpret the meaning of key terms and phrases. To achieve some understanding they often use rough translations:

> To twelve people off the street, to use the word "willful" versus "deliberate" versus "intentional"—all that becomes very foggy and gray and just sort of burns off in the sun. . . . Did he do it? Yeah. Did he mean it? Yeah. That's what people on the jury broke it down to.[62]

The key terms in the sentencing instructions are also poorly understood. One juror put it this way:

> "The first thing we asked for after the instruction was, could the judge define mitigating and aggravating circumstances. Because the different verdicts that we could come up with depended on if mitigating outweighed aggravating or if aggravating outweighed mitigating, or all of that. So we wanted to make sure. I said, 'I don't know that I exactly understand what it means.' And then everybody else said, 'No, neither do I,' or 'I can't give you a definition.' So we decided we should ask the judge. Well, the judge wrote back and said, "You have to glean it from the instructions."[63]

Judges are loath to offer any clarification beyond the vague charge of the jury instructions. When juries request further clarification about what criteria to use or how to combine the factors, most judges give a useless response: "I again will emphasize that there are no further criteria other than the instructions that have previously been given to you, and I will read the instructions to you again."[64] Judges are understandably reluctant to clarify or elaborate on the standard instructions because any alteration could later form the basis of an appeal.

Capital jurors are in special need of clear guidance. In making the logical inferences necessary to find a defendant guilty of a crime, jurors can rely on logic and evidence. But rules of logic are wholly inadequate to the task of deciding whether a defendant deserves to die. Jurors must assess the ultimate value of the person whose life hangs in the balance. What jurors can consider is restrained only by the amount of evidence presented by the attorneys and the collective capacity of the jurors to engage in complex moral inquiry. Answering the question of whether a person deserves to die for his crimes leads jurors into deep philosophical waters. They must decide when killing a defendant is justified and when it is not. The receptivity of jurors to mitigating factors is all that stands between a defendant and the execution chamber.

The guided-discretion statutes approved twenty years ago were intended to restrain the "unbridled discretion" that presumably led to a capricious, arbitrary, and discriminatory pattern of death sentencing. But if the instructions given today are not clear and informative, then it is unlikely that death sentencing is now rational and unbiased. Unfortunately, the Court's confidence in the current system is founded on their own untested (and often unstated) assumptions about the process of jury decision-making. As we shall see, research indicates that the pattern of death verdicts remains discriminatory despite the Court's efforts to restrain the discretion of jurors.

The Appeals Process

Appellate review in capital cases is uniquely complex and elaborate. Death sentences are automatically appealed to the state supreme court. This direct appeal, circumventing all lower appellate courts, is unique to capital cases. State supreme courts evaluate whether there were legal or constitutional errors at trial, and some states provide for a "proportionality review." In such reviews, the court determines if a particular death sentence is consistent with sentences imposed in similar cases. If both the conviction and the sentence are affirmed by the state supreme court, the defendant can file a petition for *certiorari* to the United States Supreme Court. This is a request for the case to be heard by the high Court based on issues raised in the direct appeal. But the Supreme Court rarely grants such requests because an important constitutional issue must be at stake.

If the defendant's direct appeal is unsuccessful, further state and federal appeals are possible. These *habeas corpus* appeals can raise issues that go beyond the trial record, including newly discovered evidence, fairness of the trial, jury bias, tainted evidence, incompetence of defense counsel, and prosecutorial misconduct. If these appeals are denied by the trial court, they may be filed with a court of appeals. State *habeas* appeals can proceed to the state supreme court and, if denied, a new petition for *certiorari* can be filed with the United States Supreme Court.

After exhausting state appeals, a defendant can file federal *habeas corpus* petitions. Appeals to federal courts must be confined to alleged violations of constitutional rights. Such rights include the right to due process (Fourteenth Amendment), the prohibition against cruel and unusual punishment (Eighth Amendment), and the right to effective assistance of counsel (Sixth Amendment). Federal petitions begin in a United States District Court and then, if denied, are taken to a federal court of appeals. Finally, appeals may be made to the United States Supreme Court on constitutional grounds. Though many forms of appeal are possible after sentencing, only the automatic review by the state supreme court is mandatory.

Federal *habeas* petitions have long been the means for reviewing (and sometimes reversing) the convictions of state courts. Independent review by federal courts has been an important safeguard against violations of basic rights and convictions of innocent persons. However, in 1996 a law was passed that severely restricts federal appeals. Instead of multiple avenues of appeal, death-row inmates will be entitled to a single comprehensive federal court review. Under the new system, if the state has a procedure for selecting and paying attorneys for death-row inmates (there is a critical shortage of lawyers willing or able to conduct such appeals), the federal petition must be filed within six months of the final state appeal.[65]

When a sentence has been upheld by the state supreme court, an execution warrant may be issued. The date of execution is generally set for not less than thirty days after the warrant has been issued. If appeals are pending, the defendant must apply for a stay of execution. The power to stay executions and commute death sentences rests with the courts, the state governor, or a board of pardons.

It is important to note that political concerns enter the process at several points. Many key decision-makers—district attorneys, judges (including state supreme court justices in some states), and state governors—are elected and usually hope to be reelected. If a district attorney decides not to seek the death penalty in a high-profile murder case, or a judge overturns a death sentence, or a governor commutes a death sentence, their political careers can be hobbled. Political opponents will use such decisions to portray the prosecutor or judge or governor as "soft on crime." That dreaded label could make the difference between victory and defeat in the next election. That is why, for example, in states that elect their supreme courts, death sentences are affirmed at a much higher rate.

Death Row

People sentenced to death are sent to death row. Located in the maximum-security units of state penitentiaries, death rows are nonetheless a world apart. Because the men (and the few women) on the row have been judged to be beyond redemption, not even halfhearted attempts at rehabilitation are made. In most states, the inhabitants of death row spend from twenty to twenty-two hours per day in their cells. For a couple of hours each day, they are free to play games and roam a concrete yard bounded by fences and razor wire.

The one commodity death-row inmates have in abundance is time. Their constant enemies are crushing boredom and loss of all hope. There is too much time to think. One observer put it this way: "The inhabitants of the row live lives that don't bear much thinking about. There's the ugly past that got them to this place, the miserable present, and the future they don't want to come."[66]

After the trial, after the appeals have been exhausted, and after long years of confinement on the row, the execution date finally arrives. The nature of life on death row, the rituals and procedures used to kill condemned prisoners, and the effects of living on death row are the subject of the next chapter.

CHAPTER THREE

Is the Death Penalty Inhumane?

I regard the death penalty as a savage and immoral institution that undermines the moral and legal foundations of society.
—*Andrei Sakharov*

On death row the allegorical pound of flesh is just the beginning. Here the whole person is consumed. The spirit is captured and gradually worn down, then the body is disposed of.
—*Robert Johnson*

Early forms of execution were certainly cruel by modern standards. Stoning, drawing and quartering, and breaking at the wheel induced terrible pain and a slow, excruciating death. Sometimes the goal was to produce as much pain as possible without bringing death, for example, when the authorities wanted to secure a confession before killing the prisoner. Modern techniques attempt to minimize the suffering of the prisoner being killed.

The three methods of execution most familiar to Americans— electrocution, poisonous gas, and lethal injection—are used only in the United States. Worldwide, hanging and shooting are still the most popular forms of execution. Beheading is also widely used, especially under Islamic law.[67] Firing squads and scaffolds are rarely seen in the United States (although there was a hanging in 1993 and a shooting in 1996), and electric chairs and gas chambers appear to be on their way out. Lethal injection may eventually become the only means of execution in the United States. As one official method of killing is abandoned for another, the argument is always that the new method is more humane.

Ropes, Bullets, Electricity, Gas, and Poison

In the early days of our country, hanging was the dominant form of execution. The goal of hanging is to snap the prisoner's spine. A noose is tightened around the neck, and a trapdoor beneath the prisoner's feet swings open. If all goes well, the cervical vertebrae are dislocated and death comes quickly. In the 1800s and earlier, though, even official, well-planned hangings were often botched. Despite the long drop, some prisoners failed to die from the fall and dangled from the end of the rope, slowly strangulating. Often the executioner would simply pull down on the hanging man's feet to finish the job. Even this spectacle was less gruesome than what happened when the prisoner was too heavy and the drop was too long. In such cases, the fall could rip the head from the body, leaving a bloody rope and a decapitated prisoner on the ground. Fortunately, modern hangings almost never go awry. Hanging in the United States is now a precise, scientific (though somewhat ghoulish) procedure: The prisoner is carefully weighed and measured, the rope is tested for strength and flexibility, the execution routine is well rehearsed, and the optimal length for the rope is carefully calculated. However, even if the hanged man has lost consciousness, the body may convulse and the heart may continue beating for a few minutes. This spectacle is disturbing to many witnesses.

Execution by firing squad can bring death by massive damage to internal organs or damage to the central nervous system or by hemorrhage. The 1996 execution of John Taylor in Utah provides a clear look at the modern method of death by shooting (Taylor claimed he was innocent and chose a firing squad over lethal injection to embarrass state officials). Taylor was strapped into a wooden armchair and a hood was placed over his head. A stethoscope was used to locate his heart and a red cloth target was pinned to the site. Five anonymous sharpshooters fired on command and Taylor died quickly. A large pan was positioned under his chair to collect the draining blood. A state official reported that in the 39 executions by firing squad it had taken anywhere from 15 seconds to 27 minutes for the prisoner to die.[68]

In 1879 Thomas Edison invented the electric lightbulb, and ten years later a condemned prisoner was electrocuted in New York. The electric chair was to replace the noose because killing by electrocution was thought to be more humane, modern, and scientific. A mysterious, invisible force would simply be passed through the prisoner's body and he would expire almost instantly. A quiet, tidy form of killing. Edison opposed capital punishment and did not want to see his "direct current" associated with killing. He recommended use of the "alternating current" advocated by his rival George Westinghouse on the grounds that it was more "dangerous."[69]

To prepare for electrocution, part of a prisoner's leg and head are shaved to afford good contact with electrodes. On the fateful day, the prisoner is strapped to the chair and a powerful surge of electricity (about 1,900 volts) is passed through his body. Although the official goal is paralysis of the heart and respiratory system due to burning of the internal organs, "the condemned prisoner often leaps forward against restraining straps when the switch is thrown; the prisoner may defecate, urinate, or vomit blood. Eye-witnesses always report that there is a smell of burned flesh."[70]

In the case of lethal gas, the prisoner is strapped to a steel chair in an airtight chamber with a stethoscope taped to the chest. The heartbeat can be monitored from an adjacent room and is used to fix the time of death. A lever outside of the death chamber is pulled to drop capsules of sodium cyanide into a vat of sulfuric acid. Cyanide gas fills the chamber, and death is caused by "asphyxiation due to inhibition by the cyanide gas of the respiratory enzymes which transfer oxygen from the blood to the body cells."[71] A sort of cellular asphyxiation.

Lethal injection is the most recent innovation in the technology of execution. First tried in 1977, it is now the most popular technique in the United States. The prisoner is strapped to a gurney on his back, and needles that will deliver the poison are inserted in both arms, usually just opposite the elbow. Three substances are injected: the first is a fast-acting anesthetic (sodium thiopentone), the second is a drug that paralyzes the diaphragm and respiratory muscles (pancuronium bromide), and the third drug stops the heart (potassium chloride).[72]

Are any of these techniques of killing truly humane? It is impossible to know. Almost no one gets out of the execution chamber alive. In 1946, because of a malfunction in the machinery of death, seventeen-year-old Willie Francis experienced a few seconds of electrocution and lived to tell about it. He said the experience was quite painful, and that "my mouth tasted like cold peanut butter. I felt a burning in my head and my left leg, and I jumped against the straps. I saw little blue and pink and green speckles."[73] A year later, Francis had his second date with the executioner. The Supreme Court was unpersuaded by his argument that it was "cruel and unusual" to execute him twice. On the second try, the execution went according to plan.

Although each of the five methods described above has been touted as especially civilized and humane at some time, no method works perfectly on every occasion. As I noted earlier, some botched hangings led to decapitation or slow strangulation, but errors are not confined to hanging. In the case of a firing squad, nervous shooters may not hit the intended target and the prisoner may bleed to death. In September of 1951, a prisoner named Elisio Mares faced a firing squad. Mares was well liked by the prison staff, and when the command to shoot came, all five sharpshooters aimed away from his heart. The bullets tore through the right side of his chest, leaving Mares to bleed to death slowly. As the British Royal Commission on Capital Punishment noted forty-five years ago, execution by firing squad "does not possess even the first requisite of an efficient method, the certainty of causing immediate death."[74]

Modern American techniques—electrocution, poisonous gas, and lethal injection—are not without problems of their own.

Botched executions can be the result of mistakes by the execution-ers, equipment problems, or struggling by the condemned pris-oner. In 1985, Alpha Otis Stephens was strapped to the electric chair in Georgia. Stephens had to be hit with three separate 1,900-volt surges of electricity. After the first surge he "struggled for breath for eight minutes." When the second surge was applied, "his body slumped when the current stopped . . . but shortly after-ward witnesses saw him struggle to breathe. In the six minutes al-lowed for the body to cool before doctors could examine it, Mr. Stephens took about 23 breaths."[75] When the doctors declared that he was still alive, a third jolt finished him off ten minutes later. His experience was not unique. Also in 1985, William Vandiver needed five separate charges of electricity and seventeen minutes to die. And, in 1990, "flames, smoke and sparks shot six inches out of the head of Jessie Tafero as three 2,000-volt shocks were admin-istered. Because the amperage was incorrect, Tafero's flesh cooked on his bones before he died."[76] And in 1991, mistakes by the execu-tion team led to a hideous spectacle in the execution of Albert Clozza. "Steam pressure in Clozza's head caused his eyeballs to pop so that blood ran down his chest from the sockets."[77] Accord-ing to Fred Leuchter, a major designer of execution machinery, the problem with electrocution is that

> if you overload an individual's body with current . . . you'll cook the meat on his body. It's like meat on an overcooked chicken. If you grab the arm, the flesh will fall right off in your hands. That doesn't mean he felt anything. It simply means that it's cosmetically not the thing to do. Presumably the state will return the remains to the victim's family for burial. Returning someone who had been cooked would be in poor taste.[78]

Once considered a humane alternative to electrocution, lethal gas is slowly being abandoned. As prisoners succumb to the ef-fects of poisonous gas, most buck and strain against the restrain-

ing straps, and many convulse for several minutes before finally
dying. In a 1995 lawsuit alleging that gassing was unnecessarily
cruel, a physician testified that "veterinarians won't even use cyanide to put dogs to sleep."[79]

There now appears to be a consensus that lethal injection is the
most humane method of killing. Although it is impossible to know
for sure, the consensus is probably correct. Based on external indi-
cators of pain and distress (i.e., screaming, sweating, facial grimaces,
defecation and urination, vomiting, pupil dilation, writhing of the
body), one neurobiologist has concluded that injection probably
causes the least suffering.[80] However, such signs are imperfect in-
dicators of pain, since leather restraints and the effects of muscle re-
laxants suppress movements of the face and body.

Usually, the injection of deadly chemicals goes smoothly—no
violent convulsing of the body, no mutilated corpse. Yet there are
problems even with this most sanitized form of execution. If the
prisoner has a history of intravenous drug use, the executioner
may have to use surgery to locate a suitable deeper vein. If the
prisoner struggles for his life, insertion of the needle can be difficult and painful. Technical problems are also possible. The lethal drugs can be improperly combined, the drugs may thicken
and clog the delivery tube or needle, the anesthetic may not take
effect immediately. Such problems prolong the process of killing.
In 1984, a clogged catheter caused James Autry to remain conscious, struggling and complaining about pain for about ten
minutes. In 1988, the syringe popped out of Raymond Landry's
arm, spewing lethal chemicals toward witnesses. He was not pronounced dead until twenty-four minutes after the drugs began to
flow. Lethal injection also allows for a more insidious type of
botched execution: a painful, lingering death that *appears* to be
painless and swift. When injecting the lethal drugs, "even a small
error in dosage or administration can leave a prisoner conscious
but paralyzed while dying, a sentient witness of his or her own
slow, lingering asphyxiation."[81]

Because lethal injection is probably the most humane way of killing prisoners, people in the anti–death penalty camp have come to favor the needle over the rope, the bullet, the electric chair, and the gas chamber. But the switch to the syringe has had the unintended consequence of making executions seem almost civilized. A man lying faceup on a hospital gurney is subjected to what looks like a routine medical procedure. The only difference is that the goal is to kill instead of heal. In the distant past, executions were savage spectacles. Modern American techniques mute this savagery, although the occasional botched execution still calls up associations with the barbaric rituals of the past. Luckily, as the injection technology is refined and improved, repulsive displays of prisoners writhing in agony will probably become even rarer. Killing by the state will be swift, simple, sanitized, and maybe even more humane. Even more important from the perspective of politicians and proponents of the death penalty is that lethal injection is the method least likely to arouse doubts or revulsion in the minds of the public. The new technology will anesthetize the public conscience along with the condemned man.

Between Sentencing and Execution: Life on Death Row

Death row is a prison within a prison. It is a special area of the prison designed to hold inmates who are waiting to be killed. It is little more than a warehouse, a massive holding tank, a storage facility for people awaiting their appointment with the executioner. Death rows are usually housed in the maximum-security sections of major state penitentiaries, in an area segregated from the general prison population. Because very few inmates will get out of death row alive (some will be executed, many will have their sentences overturned, many will die natural deaths), there is no attempt to educate, rehabilitate, or in any way improve the residents of the row. The conditions of confinement are far more restrictive than those of the general prison population. With a

few notable exceptions (see Chapter 9), there is no access to train-
ing programs or prison work.

Most death-row inmates spend about twenty-one hours a day
in a six-by-nine foot cell. In the cell are usually a toilet, a sink, a
narrow bed, and a small metal locker. If you tore out the bathtub
in your family bathroom and replaced it with a bed, you would
have something a bit nicer than an average cell on death row.
Imagine spending the next ten years of your life in your reconstructed bathroom. Each day you have 24 hours to fill; each week
you have 168 hours. Even if you eat your meals very slowly and
sleep 10 hours per day, there are still hundreds of days and
thousands of hours to fill each year. The idleness, monotony, and
relentless boredom are enough to unravel the sanity of most men.

Three times a day, the occupants of death row receive a meal
through a slot in their cell door. Twice a week they are locked
into a metal cage with a shower head for a ten-minute shower.
Perhaps two or three hours a day they are permitted to go out-
doors to a fenced-in concrete area known as "the yard." At night
the lights in the cells are dimmed, but the lights in the corridor
still burn brightly. Ventilation is poor, and the air is stagnant and
full of the smells of men who seldom shower as well as the smells
from scores of toilets. It is too hot in summer, too cold in winter,
and it is almost always noisy. Men yell to one another through
the bars, radios and televisions play, rolling carts clatter through
the corridors, steel doors slam shut.

Television is the primary diversion on many death rows, and the
presence of TV serves the interests of the prison staff. A journalist
who has written extensively about death row puts it this way:

> God, it drives the hard-liners in the legislature and the fire-
> brands of talk radio crazy to think that prisoners on death
> row have TV sets in their cells. Coddling the criminals!
> Indulging them with luxuries! It would be hard to find a
> prison guard, though, who opposed the sets. Television is

the only thing that makes death row manageable. The prison staff has a special nickname for those TV sets . . . "electronic tranquilizers."[82]

One inmate refers to TV as a "psychic club" used to pacify the inmates on death row. It is also a powerful bargaining tool; few inmates are willing to risk loss of their precious television by failing to follow the rules.

Another factor that shapes life on death row is the interest in maintaining security. Of course, all prisons have strong concerns about security, but these concerns are magnified on death row. Such worries are legitimate; if a prisoner were able to smuggle in a weapon, the results could be disastrous. Prison workers are fond of telling stories about ingenious attempts to smuggle in contraband. Two different prison workers told me that one prisoner's girlfriend swallowed a small balloon filled with drugs just prior to her visit. Once in the visiting room, she managed to regurgitate the balloon and pass it into the mouth of the prisoner by means of a kiss. According to the guards, the prisoner then swallowed the balloon and later retrieved the drugs from his own feces.

Prior to a scheduled visit, visitors must pass through a metal detector and undergo a thorough search. Often, prisoners must submit to a "body-cavity strip search." Mumia Abu-Jamal, a death-row inmate in Pennsylvania, offers a succinct description of the degrading procedure:

Once the prisoner is naked, the visiting-room guard spits out a familiar cadence:
"Open yer mouth.
"Stick out your tongue.
"You wear any dentures?
"Lemme see both sides of you hands.
"Pull your foreskin back.
"Lift you sac.

"Turn around.
"Bend over.
"Spread your cheeks.
"Bottom of yer feet.
"Get dressed."[83]

Security is also the official reason for the policy of "noncontact visits" in some death rows. Though security is the rationale for prohibiting contact, the effect is to isolate the prisoner further from his loved ones. The noted psychiatrist Karl Menninger called the noncontact visit needlessly cruel and "a violation of ordinary principles of humanity." Abu-Jamal described a heart-wrenching noncontact visit with his young daughter.

> She burst into the tiny visiting room, her brown eyes aglitter with happiness; stopped, stunned, staring at the glassy barrier between us; and burst into tears. . . . In milliseconds, sadness and shock shifted into fury as her petite fingers curled into tight fists, which banged and pummeled the Plexiglas barrier, which shuddered and shimmied but didn't shatter. "Break it! Break it!" she screamed. Her mother, recovering from her shock, bundled up Hamida in her arms, as sobs rocked them both. . . . "Why can't I hug him? Why can't we kiss? Why can't I sit in his lap? Why can't we touch? Why not?"[84]

Many, if not most, death-row inmates slowly lose their ties to the outside world. The family of the inmates—who are uniformly poor—often cannot afford to miss work or spend the money to make the long trip to prisons that are located far from population centers. Visits are difficult and painful for most loved ones, and, over a period of years, visitors arrive far less often or not at all. And there are greatly diminished opportunities to form relationships with guards or other inmates. Guards assigned to death row "shall avoid any personal discussions," instructs a manual for death-row staffers. "Employees must not be too familiar or discuss personal items of interest with the inmates."[85]

Social scientists, death-row inmates, and prison guards have long attempted to identify the essential features of life on death row: Loss of control over all aspects of life, an almost total loss of privacy, loneliness and isolation, crushing boredom, enforced idleness, vulnerability to prison staff and other inmates. Although these are features of prison life in general, pain and privation are amplified on the row. Visits are less frequent and more restrictive, opportunities for work or education range from none to few, there is far less out-of-cell time, there are few opportunities to form friendships, and, most important, there is the agonizing knowledge that the state intends to kill you.

Waiting for the Executioner

Just prior to his retirement from the Supreme Court, Justice Harry Blackmun declared his opposition to capital punishment. He described lethal injection in graphic terms: "Intravenous tubes attached to his arms will carry the instrument of death, a toxic fluid designed specifically for the purpose of killing human beings." Justice Antonin Scalia countered by recounting the brutal rape and murder of an eleven-year-old: "How enviable a quiet death by lethal injection compared with that!"[86] he wrote. And, of course, he is right. Compared to nearly all capital murders, the state's killing is clean and humane. Even the most efficient murder—a bullet that rips through the chest or the head—is far more brutal and painful than a meticulously planned killing carried out by the state. But an execution can only be considered humane if we confine our view to the act of execution. It is the cruel preliminaries that produce the most pain. As Albert Camus put it:

> For there to be equivalence, the death penalty would have to punish a criminal who had warned his victim of the date at

which he would inflict a horrible death on him and who, from that moment onward, had confined him at his mercy for months. Such a monster is not encountered in private life.[87]

The moment of execution is only the final moment in a long process that begins with sentencing. Once the death sentence is pronounced, the prisoner knows that he will die in prison—either he will be killed there or he will die there of natural causes. Because of the possibilities of a new trial, or a successful appeal, or a commuted sentence, the moods of death-row inmates are likely to swing between mild hope and abject despair. The criminologist Robert Johnson has made an extensive study of death row and the execution process. He found that death-row inmates are tormented by intrusive thoughts about their impending execution. They imagine how they will behave in the hours and minutes leading up to their death, they speculate about the pain of being executed, they wonder if their legs will collapse under them as they walk to the death chamber. Many are haunted by recurring nightmares about their execution and about 70 percent suffer from severe depression and symptoms of psychosis.

> I sit in that cell, you know, and it seems like I'm just ready to scream or go crazy or something. . . . I sit up at night, you know. You just sit there, and it seems like things are closing in on you. Like last night, when I sit in there and everything's real quiet, just a buzzing noise gets to going in my ears. And I sit there, and I consciously think, "Am I going crazy?" And the buzzing gets louder; and you sit there and you want to scream.[88]

Condemned men also ruminate about how the execution and the publicity surrounding it will affect their fathers, mothers, spouses, siblings, and children. A psychiatrist who worked with the condemned concluded that confinement on death row "invariably results in claustrophobia, and often results in chronic anxiety and depression. Prisoners . . . eventually lose the will to live. The prolonged confinement in a small cell with a light kept burning by night could be regarded as a form of psychological torture."[89] If torture, as defined by the United Nations, consists of "severe pain or suffering, whether physical or mental," then waiting for several years on death row for an appointment with the executioner surely qualifies as psychological torture. According to the testimonies of torture survivors around the world, "The threat of execution is one of the most terrifying forms of torture."[90] To make the abstract threat real, occasionally a fellow resident of the row is taken from his cell and escorted to the execution chamber. Indeed, many condemned prisoners become so despondent that they decide to abandon further appeals and ask the state to carry out the execution. They submit to a sort of state-sponsored suicide. Death starts to seem like the only way to escape their miserable existence.

The Execution Ritual

For most Americans the death penalty is an abstract topic of debate. From a safe distance, we demand that it be carried out. We don't really want to be bothered by the details. But for a few prison workers, and a few witnesses, an execution is a vivid, personal, real event. Some prison workers claim to be unmoved by executions. One member of an "execution team" put it this way:

I can take or leave executions. It's not a job I like or dislike. It's a job I've been asked to do. . . . If they would stop the death penalty, it wouldn't bother me. If we had ten executions tomorrow, it wouldn't bother me. I would condition my mind to get me through it.[91]

Every step in the execution process, from the issuing of the death warrant to the time when the corpse is carried out of the death chamber, is spelled out in meticulous detail. Twenty-four hours prior to the execution, the prisoner is moved to a special cell next to the chamber, two guards are posted outside the cell to prevent the prisoner from committing suicide and "to move him through a series of critical and cumulatively demoralizing junctures beginning with his last meal and ending with his last walk."[92] This is the "deathwatch." There is a final visit with loved ones, the prisoner is served a last meal, his meager personal possessions are boxed for distribution to relatives after the execution, a "spiritual adviser" is allowed to visit, a final shower is taken, the prisoner is dressed in a clean execution uniform, a photograph is taken, the death warrant is read aloud. If death is to be caused by electrocution, the head and right leg are shaved to ensure good contact with the electrodes; if poisonous gas is to be used, cyanide capsules are bagged in cheesecloth so that they can be lowered into the bowl of acid; and if the killing is to be accomplished by lethal injection, several syringes are prepared: 20cc of sterile saline solution, 50cc of potassium chloride, 50cc of pancuronium bromide, and 5 grams of sodium pentothal.[93]

Each member of the "execution team"—the prison officials who actually prepare for and carry out the execution—has a specific and limited duty: to watch the prisoner for a six-hour shift, to escort the prisoner on his final walk to the chamber, to tighten one or more of the leather straps that hold the prisoner to a chair or gurney. Responsibility for the killing is diffused among several members of the team. According to one commentator, the bureaucratic ritual leading up to the moment of execution

arose as a necessary device to keep order in the prison around the time of an execution, to keep the execution party's mind off the grisliness of their task over a period as long as ten days, and to control the condemned man's fear by making him believe he was a part of a ritual that was being conducted in a competent way by trained people. . . .[94]

In his moving book *Death Work*, Robert Johnson notes that very few condemned prisoners have to be forcibly dragged to the execution chamber. Condemned men have already been tamed and exhausted by years of confinement. Something resembling emotional death has already been accomplished and all that remains is to kill the body. "The officials' goal, and in the end perhaps the prisoner's as well, is a smooth, orderly, and ostensibly voluntary execution, one that looks humane and dignified and is not sullied in any way by obvious violence."[95] To win the cooperation of the prisoner, guards help him through the ritual, attend to his needs, and try to keep his mind off the impending execution. And "the prisoner, obviously in distress, is admonished to walk to his death like a man, in conformity with the official script; the executioners, in control of themselves and the situation, imply that, in exchange, they will do the job cleanly and without a hitch."[96] As one official put it, "I seen most of them right there at the end. They weaken to the point where they'll be almost crying, and I tell them, I say, 'Well, you don't want to go out like that.' I say, 'People be here in a minute—pull yourself up.' . . . That works every time for me."[97]

The people responsible for the execution must not only try to induce the prisoner to meet his death without resistance or incident, they must also psych themselves up for their grim task. Johnson found that members of the execution team prepared themselves by thinking about the horrible crime committed by the condemned man. As one prison officer put it, "You read the papers and things, and you brush up on the case and just see what this man has done, you know . . . you try to find out all the dirty things that he done. So, so you say, 'Well, okay, it's okay. It's all right, all right to put him to death.' "[98]

The rules and procedures designed, in part, to prevent the

prison staff from feeling sympathy for condemned inmates some-times fail. Those assigned to carry out executions are sometimes deeply affected by the experience. Donald Cabana, a former prison warden, described an execution he presided over as the most difficult experience of his life. He also described the burden placed on other prison workers: "I watched the terrible pain of guards who had worked for eight years with this young man and who would turn their face from you, not in shame, but because they didn't want you to see the emotions and the pain and the burden on them. I could see the stress and pressure that was bearing down on all of them."[99] Cabana writes that prison officials must believe that "people can and do change" and that

this young black man arrived on death row as an 18-year-old who was embittered, a drug addict, and feeling sorry for himself. The young man I was going to be asked to execute was so very different. He was at peace with himself, he was at peace with the world, and he was at peace with his God. . . . I had watched a human being change before my eyes over the course of eight years, a person who had become a different and far better person, in many respects far better than me or than many people I knew.[100]

The burden and strain of carrying out a death sentence reaches beyond prison personnel, the family of the victim, and the family of the condemned. It is also felt by investigators, police officers, prosecuting attorneys, defense attorneys, jurors, and judges, all of whom must devote considerable time and effort either to block or to clear the way for an execution. The emotional toll can be heavy. Even journalists who witness the execution report some short-term symptoms of stress, including crying, listlessness, in-ability to concentrate, and nightmares.[101]

Participation in the execution process sometimes includes physicians and psychiatrists. Because the first principle of medical ethics is "Do no harm," the involvement of medical personnel in executions is a fundamental breach of medical ethics. Such involvement is opposed by every national medical association. In 1991, Illinois passed a law requiring the presence of two physicians during lethal injections. To entice physicians into the process of killing, the state guaranteed that it would conceal their identities and pay them in cash. The law was vigorously opposed by the American Medical Association, the American Association for the Advancement of Science, the American College of Physicians, the American Public Health Association, Physicians for Human Rights, and three major state medical associations.[102] By 1992, the law had been changed to limit the involvement of physicians to pronouncing death. Even this limited role poses a fundamental ethical dilemma. Inevitably, some men have yet to expire when the physician is called in to pronounce death. The physician must then signal the executioner to continue electrocuting, gassing, or injecting.

The existence of the death penalty makes other medical grotesqueries necessary. No condemned man is allowed to cheat the executioner by committing suicide. Indeed, if the man is physically sick or insane, medical professionals must restore him to health before they turn him over to the executioner. Hours before his scheduled execution in 1995, death-row inmate Robert Beecher managed to take an overdose of sedatives in an apparent suicide attempt. He was rushed to the hospital where his stomach was pumped, and once he fully regained consciousness, he was strapped to a gurney and killed by lethal injection. His execution was delayed only two hours. In 1991 Donald Gaskin tried to end his life by slashing his wrists and elbows, but only succeeded in passing out from loss of blood. A physician was called in to stitch up the wounds and Gaskin was strapped to a gurney in his cell and, when he regained consciousness, he was escorted to the electric chair. By law, the condemned prisoner must be fully aware of his execution and the reasons for it. This means that psychiatrists and other mental health professionals are also put in an ethical bind. Their testimony at trial about the mental capacity and competence of the capital defendant may lead to a death sentence. And once a death sentence is handed down, other mental health professionals may be asked to certify that the condemned prisoner is competent to be executed.

Cruelty from a Safe Distance

We can demand that murderers be killed, but few of us would want to do the killing. Most Americans support the death penalty in the abstract, but few juries are willing to actually impose it when faced with a living, breathing, though vicious and deeply flawed, human being. We simply want the government to take care of it, cleanly and efficiently, in a distant prison in the dead of night. Yet, by demanding that killers be killed, we place a great burden on jurors, lawyers, judges, prison officials, the families of condemned men, and even on the families of victims. More and more people are pulled into the circle of suffering. By demanding an eye for an eye we create the necessity for death rows where the conditions of confinement and waiting for death amount to a form of slow torture. Like the slow drip of the Chinese water torture, the threat of death slowly steals away the sanity of condemned men.

You may feel that it is morally acceptable to kill murderers. But is it morally acceptable to subject them to psychological torture before we kill them? And, most important, what does it say about us and our society? As Fyodor Dostoyevsky wrote, "A society should be judged not by how it treats its outstanding citizens but by how it treats its worst criminals."

CHAPTER FOUR

Is the Death Penalty Cheaper than Life Imprisonment?

Why should the taxpayers have to pay to keep this guy alive in prison for the rest of his life?

—*Juror in capital murder trial*

D isagreements about the death penalty usually turn on issues of fairness, morality, and effectiveness. But there is also the question of money. Although a purely economic analysis might be considered vulgar or irrelevant to discussion of a life-or-death issue, assertions about financial cost often emerge in debates about the value of the death penalty.

In centuries past, people found guilty of hanging crimes were escorted to the gallows within days of being convicted. Reckoning was swift and cheap. The cost of the death penalty was a modest fee paid to the executioner plus the cost of erecting a scaffold. But things have changed. As American society evolved, our system of capital punishment has been reshaped by concerns about fairness, consistency, morality, and the possibility of wrongful conviction. As a result, the death penalty is no longer swift or cheap.

Proponents of capital punishment sometimes claim that killing murderers saves the money of overburdened taxpayers. Some Americans say they support capital punishment because they believe it is cheaper to execute a condemned prisoner than to imprison that person for the remainder of his or her natural life. Questions of cost even surface when jurors are deciding whether to sentence a particular defendant to death.[103] On its face, this belief seems reasonable; surely by killing condemned prisoners we save years or even decades of costs associated with room and board. Prison is expensive, and a young murderer could live for decades after conviction. Yet, despite the intuitive appeal of the cheaper-to-execute notion, it is mistaken.

The Price Tag

To be sure, the cost of life imprisonment without parole (LWOP)—the alternative to a death sentence—is very high. A full accounting of the cost of LWOP must include the construction, financing, and operation costs of a maximum-security cell. The annualized costs of building and operating such a cell are approximately $5,000, and the cost of maintaining a maximum-security prisoner is approximately $20,000 per year.[104] Taking into account the average age of incarceration for someone convicted of homicide (30.8 years) and the average life expectancy for males in U.S. prisons, Raymond Paternoster has estimated that the total cost of LWOP ranges from $750,000 to $1.1 million per prisoner.[105] Actual costs could be substantially reduced if prisoners serving life sentences worked while in prison. That is, murderers could work to reduce the cost of their own confinement. This is already done in a limited way—many prisoners perform custodial work and some even produce products for prison-based industries—but it could be done more extensively.

Given the high price of imprisonment, it is possible to imagine a hypothetical case where an execution might be less expensive than life imprisonment. For example, if a healthy twenty-year-old was sentenced to prison and died of natural causes sixty years later, it *might* be more expensive than if he had been sentenced to death and refused to appeal his sentence. But such hypothetical cases miss the point: Cost estimates must include the cost of financing our system of capital punishment. It is not the cost of a particular case that is relevant, it is the full cost of sustaining an elaborate death-penalty system that consumes substantial time and resources and hangs like a weight on our criminal courts.

Although the cost of LWOP is high, the cost of capital punishment is far higher. In California, our most populous state, it is estimated that taxpayers could save $90 million annually by abolishing the death penalty.[106] Between 1977 and 1996, California spent more than $1 billion on its death penalty but managed to execute only five men. One of the men asked to be killed. In New York, the Department of Correctional Services calculated that reinstatement of the death penalty would cost the state $118 million each year.[107]

Even the per-execution cost is enormous. In Florida, the average cost is $3.2 million.[108] In Wisconsin, the Legislative Fiscal Bureau has estimated that reinstating the death penalty would cost the state between $1.6 million and $3.2 million per execution.[109] In California, capital trials are six times more expensive than other murder trials.[110] Texas kills more condemned prisoners than any other state and it is also the state that has done the most to minimize the time between trial and execution. Yet even in Texas each capital case costs taxpayers an average of $2.3 million, nearly three times the cost of imprisonment in a maximum-security cell for forty years.[111] Texas spent more than $183 million on the death penalty during a six-year period.[112] Harris County (which includes the city of Houston) has the dubious distinction of leading the country in the number of capital trials. In 1994, Harris County commissioners attempted to raise taxes to cover the staggering costs of capital trials. Angry voters rejected the tax hike, so fire and ambulance services had to be cut instead. Harris County is not alone. Capital trials create a crushing financial burden for many counties because counties bear a disproportionate share of the costs. James Reichle, district attorney of Sierra County, California, put it succinctly:

If we didn't have to pay $500,000 a pop for Sacramento's murderers, I'd have an investigator and the sheriff would have a couple of extra deputies and we could do some lasting good for Sierra County law enforcement.[113]

In the most thorough investigation of cost to date, Phillip Cook and Donna Slawson collected data on cost for each phase of the legal process in North Carolina. Their conclusion: Compared to first-degree murder cases in which the death penalty is not sought, the *extra* cost of adjudicating a capital case through to execution is $2.16 million.[114] But this figure underestimates the true cost because it includes only costs to state and local government (excluding all private and federal costs).

Of course, we spend time as well as money. Both the California and Florida supreme courts spend roughly half their time reviewing death-penalty cases.[115] This means that state supreme courts don't have enough time to resolve important issues affecting civil and criminal law. Personnel from state attorney generals' offices also spend considerable time responding to appeals, and governors must spend time reviewing requests to commute death sentences.

While supporters of the death penalty may quibble with the cost estimates from a particular study, the bottom line is clear: Maintaining a system of capital punishment is far more expensive than sending murderers to prison until they die of natural causes. No systematic study has reached a contrary conclusion. Even if the debilitating cost of the death penalty could be cut by half— a very unlikely event—it would still be the more expensive option. Clearly, whatever benefits Americans receive from maintaining a system of capital punishment come at a very high price. The punishment of death punishes taxpayers and drains away precious resources from the criminal justice system.

Why the Death Penalty Is So Costly

One reason that maintaining the death penalty is so expensive is that capital trials are more complex and time-consuming than other criminal trials at every stage in the legal process: crime investigation, pretrial preparation, jury selection, guilt trial, penalty trial, and appeals. Most of the money is spent early in the process—on preparing for and conducting the capital murder trial.

Trial preparation begins when the district attorney's office decides to seek the death penalty. A competently conducted capital trial requires a thorough investigation of both the crime and the offender. Because of the penalty phase, pretrial investigators will attempt to locate and interview anyone who may be able to offer testimony that can serve as mitigating evidence (e.g., members of the defendant's family, friends, co-workers, neighbors, and teachers). The personal history of the defendant is painstakingly reconstructed in an effort to explain the defendant's crime. Investigations in capital cases take three to five times longer than noncapital murder investigations and carefully conducted investigations frequently take as long as two years to complete. The use of various experts—mental health professionals, polygraphers, medical experts, forensic scientists, and jury-selection consultants—also adds to the costs. Finally, pretrial motions (i.e., requests for a ruling from the judge on various legal issues) are numerous and complex. Capital cases typically involve the filing of two to six times as many motions as noncapital cases.[116]

The process of selecting jurors also takes longer in capital trials. Few prospective jurors are able or willing to commit themselves to participating in a trial that may last for weeks or months. Attorneys in capital cases are permitted to excuse more jurors than usual for no stated reason and are given greater latitude in questioning potential jurors. Thus, jury pools must be larger. In many states, jurors are questioned individually so that their answers will not influence other potential jurors. As noted in Chapter 2, capital trials include the added complication of death qualification. Finally, attorneys take more time during *voir dire* because jurors are being selected for two trials—a guilt trial and a separate penalty trial. For these reasons, jury selection takes about five times longer in capital trials than in noncapital murder trials.[117]

Attorneys in capital cases must investigate and prepare for a charge of first-degree murder *and* other felony charges that qualify the offense as capital (e.g., rape or robbery). Because of the enormous workload, both defense and prosecution teams usually include two attorneys and many investigators. The need to formulate a guilt-phase strategy that complements the penalty-phase strategy further complicates the job of prosecutors and defenders. Capital guilt phases consume ten to twenty times as many attorney labor-hours as noncapital cases, and capital trials generally last three times longer than comparable noncapital trials.[118] Most important, the extra costs associated with capital trials are incurred not only when a defendant is sentenced to death, but also when a defendant is acquitted or sentenced to life imprisonment. Since only a minority of capital offenders are sentenced to death—estimates range from less than 30 percent to only 10 percent[119]—most of the money that is spent to maintain our system of capital punishment is spent on the lengthy, expensive trials of defendants who end up being sentenced to life imprisonment. Thus, the cost per death sentence is astronomical.

Although most of the money spent on capital punishment is spent before appeals even begin, the labyrinthine appeals process for capital cases is also expensive. Estimates of the cost of appealing a single capital case range from $170,000 to $219,000.[120] Capital appeals generally cost more than noncapital appeals because of the complexity of the legal issues involved, the number of different issues that can be raised, and the availability of multiple avenues for appeal. Because a high proportion of appeals in capital cases are successful, and because the defendant's life is at stake, there is ample incentive for pursuing every avenue of appeal. When an appeal is successful, the state must bear the cost of fighting the death sentence *as well as* the cost of imprisoning the convict for life. This is the key to understanding the true cost of the death penalty: We pay the high price of a capital trial *not only* when a defendant is sentenced to death, but *also* when a defendant is acquitted or sentenced to life imprisonment. And only about three out of every ten capital cases culminate in a sentence of death. For the minority of defendants who do receive a death sentence, we pay for an expensive capital trial *and* an expensive appeals process. When an appeal is successful, the state bears the cost of fighting the death sentence *in addition to* the cost of life imprisonment.

Finally, the price tag for capital punishment includes the considerable expense of operating death rows. Death row is an expensive maximum-security unit within a large penitentiary. As many analysts have noted, the demands of running a death row create problems for prison officials. "Without the sentence of death, the condemned would not necessarily be the most dangerous prison inmates demanding the limited single cells available for strict security. In consequence, the prison system is severely restricted in its ability to find secure space for its own troublemakers."[121] The mere existence of death row has an unsettling effect on the entire prison population, and during the days preceding and following a scheduled execution, disruptive behavior by inmates peaks.

Compared to the massive costs of capital trials, appeals, and incarceration on death row, the cost of building, maintaining, and operating an execution chamber is only a tiny drop in a large bucket. But it is worth mentioning. The chamber and the additional personnel time needed to run the execution machinery and to prepare the condemned prisoner for death also add to the cost.

The majority of defendants accused of capital crimes do not die in the execution chamber. Some aren't convicted, many are convicted but not sentenced to death, many have their sentence reversed on appeal, a few have their death sentences commuted, and others die before being marched to the execution chamber.

Still, the vast and intricate procedural machinery of capital punishment must continue to be financed. Massive resources are squandered, courts and prisons are strained, just so that, eventually, a few condemned prisoners can be killed. Whatever satisfaction we receive from executions must be weighed against the time and money spent to sustain our system of capital punishment.

The true price of the death penalty looms even larger when one considers what economists call "opportunity costs"—in this case, the value of what could have been purchased if the death penalty had not been purchased. Put differently, the tremendous sums of money expended each year to maintain a system of capital punishment could be spent more productively elsewhere, for example, on programs designed to prevent or suppress crime. In recent years, many states have been forced to take extraordinary steps to deal with shrinking budgets. Early intervention and education programs have been cut, and violent offenders have been released early from prisons. Yet capital punishment has been spared by budget cutters. By focusing on killing a handful of individual offenders, we divert precious attention and millions of dollars away from reforms that address the causes of violent crime.

Streamlining the System to Cut Costs

Must our system of capital punishment be so time-consuming and expensive? Can the system be simplified, thereby reducing its total cost? Some streamlining has already occurred. Our current Supreme Court has rendered a series of decisions limiting the scope and variety of postconviction appeals.[122] In 1996, limits on federal appeals went into effect. It is not yet clear whether these new limits will reduce the cost of appeals at the federal level. One possible consequence is that the appellate battles will be shifted to state courts and states will bear a greater proportion of the costs. Many have argued that justice and our ability to detect errors have already been severely compromised by recent reforms. Further streamlining is unwise and unlikely for several reasons.

First, in fashioning a system of capital jurisprudence that passes constitutional muster, the United States Supreme Court has repeatedly emphasized that the punishment of death is qualitatively different from all other punishments, because of its severity and irrevocability. This "death is different" doctrine holds that capital defendants are entitled to what has been called "super due process." This includes the trial and appeals procedures discussed above. As Justice O'Connor has observed:

> Among the most important and consistent themes in the Court's death penalty jurisprudence is the need for special care and deliberation in decisions that may lead to the imposition of that sanction. The Court has accordingly imposed a series of unique substantive and procedural restrictions designed to ensure that capital punishment is not imposed without the serious and calm reflection that ought to precede any decision of such gravity and finality.[123]

The unique procedural safeguards alluded to by Justice O'Connor include separate guilt and penalty trials, great latitude in presenting mitigating evidence during the penalty trial, automatic appeal to the state supreme court, and a greater number and variety of opportunities for judicial review of death sentences. The current system was developed over several decades in an effort to increase fairness and to prevent arbitrary or discriminatory sentences of death. There is no bargain-basement version of justice in death-penalty cases. Any further attempt to bypass these safeguards would violate the constitutional rights of the defendant, exacerbate racially discriminatory death sentencing, and increase the number of innocent people sent to the execution chamber.

A second argument against streamlining the current system is that a substantial number of capital convictions and death sentences are overturned on appeal because of errors. That is, because of mistakes at the initial trial, appeals courts often reduce death sentences to LWOP. For example, 48 percent of direct appeals to the Florida Supreme Court resulted in reversals of either sentence or conviction,[124] and the Georgia Supreme Court overturned 20 percent of the death sentences reviewed on direct appeal.[125] The South Carolina Supreme Court reversed 37 percent of death sentences and 29 percent of convictions for capital crimes.[126] Overall, the rate of reversal for capital cases is about six times higher than the rate of reversals for noncapital cases. A streamlined system would fail to catch and correct these errors.

The appellate success rate at the federal level is similarly high. In one study, federal appellate courts ruled for the capital defendant in 73 percent of *habeas* petitions, whereas the courts ruled for the defendant in only 6 percent of noncapital cases.[127] More recent estimates are that about 40 percent of federal appeals in capital cases are successful while only 2 percent of noncapital appeals are successful.[128] Some people believe that these reversals can be attributed to trivial legal technicalities. But the best research available suggests that most reversals result from gross error or fundamental violations of constitutional rights, e.g., ineffective assistance of counsel, jury misconduct, and fabricated evidence.[129] Indeed, if the error is ruled to be "harmless" then there is no reversal.

There are many possible explanations for the high rate of reversal in death-penalty cases. More errors may occur in capital cases because public outrage and media attention create pressure for a speedy conviction. Public defenders or court-appointed attorneys are often overworked or inexperienced in capital cases. Prosecutors may pursue the death penalty in questionable cases as a means of advancing their own careers. Judges may simply be more willing to reverse a sentence of death because it is uniquely severe.

The enhanced procedural protections afforded the capital defendant are designed to eliminate error—to ensure that only those guilty of the most egregious crimes are sentenced to death. If errors had in fact been eliminated, then perhaps the entire system could be streamlined without increasing the risk of error. Unfortunately, the available data suggest that even our current elaborate system permits significant errors. The most troubling form of error in capital cases is the conviction, imprisonment, or execution of an innocent person. Of course, our criminal justice system is far from infallible and there is strong evidence that such extreme miscarriages of justice do occur—more on that later. Even the most ardent supporters of capital punishment do not want to increase the probability of convicting or executing innocent defendants.

In sum, there is considerable evidence that Americans will save money when the death penalty is abolished. Streamlining the legal system might reduce costs, but the moral consequences of streamlining (e.g., violations of constitutional rights, increased capriciousness, a rise in wrongful convictions and executions) are unacceptably high. Capital punishment as social program must be defended or challenged on the basis of a cost-benefit analysis. In the absence of compelling evidence that the death penalty reduces violent crime and makes our streets safer, wise policy-makers should choose the cheaper option of LWOP and spend the savings on crime prevention. This would ease the strain on the legal system, prevent the execution of innocents, and free up some of the resources poured into our current system of capital punishment.

CHAPTER FIVE

Is the Death Penalty Fairly Applied?

Till the infallibility of human judgment shall have been proved
to me, I shall demand the abolition of the death penalty.
—*Marquis de Lafayette*

In 1995 Orenthal James Simpson went on trial for the savage
murder of his former wife, Nicole Brown Simpson, and her
friend Ronald Goldman. Mr. Simpson was handsome and charm-
ing, a record-setting football hero, a persuasive pitchman for several products, and a sometime movie actor. Most important, he
was a multimillionaire.

One of the first decisions faced by the L.A. district attorney's
office was whether to seek the death penalty. They decided not
to. That decision was certainly reasonable. Mr. Simpson had no
prior felony convictions and, because one of the victims was the
mother of his two young children, executing him would have
made the children orphans. He was also a beloved celebrity, a
hero to many Americans. It would have been difficult to persuade
a jury to sentence O. J. to die by execution. Also, political pressures may have been decisive. The DA had been elected with
strong support from the black community and leaders in that
community made it clear that they would prefer that the death
penalty not be at stake. Finally, seeking the death penalty is rare;
the Los Angeles District Attorney's Office decides to seek the
ultimate penalty in only 16 percent of eligible cases.[130]

But, as many critics of the decision pointed out at the time,
prosecutors could also have found reasons for pursuing an execution. There were, after all, two victims, and both of their
throats had been brutally slashed, leaving them nearly decapitated. One of the victims had no personal relationship with the

defendant. There was also a history of violence: Simpson had been arrested as a teenager, he had pleaded no contest to a charge of spousal abuse five years earlier, and there was clear evidence of recurrent wife beating. The history of violence, the vicious nature of the crime, and the number of victims might have been used to justify a decision to seek the death penalty. My point is not that prosecutors should have tried to have Mr. Simpson killed. This book argues against the death penalty. The point is that wealth and position tipped the scales of justice in Mr. Simpson's favor from the very earliest stages in the process.

A decision not to seek an execution changes the dynamics of the case. Jurors in capital cases must be "death qualified"; prospective jurors who claim that they are incapable of voting for a sentence of death are automatically excused from service (see Chapter 2). Because death-qualified jurors tend to be more conviction prone than those not death qualified, the probability of an acquittal is increased when prosecutors decide not to seek the death penalty.

Perhaps the decision not to seek the death penalty for O. J. Simpson had nothing to do with the wealth of the defendant. But other decisions surely did. Simpson's preliminary hearing began just three weeks after the murder. The hearing was much lengthier than most, with defense attorneys vigorously asserting the rights of their client. Within four months, the trial had commenced. Eleven defense lawyers appeared in court on behalf of O. J. Simpson, and more worked behind the scenes. The full defense team also included private investigators, jury-selection consultants, and several highly paid expert witnesses who challenged every claim made by the prosecution and presented alternative interpretations of the evidence. Huge amounts of time and money were poured into the trial—it lasted nearly nine months and produced over 45,000 pages of testimony. The total cost for the defense was estimated to be somewhere between $6 million and $8 million. The final verdict was "not guilty."

All the Justice Money Can Buy

In an appearance on *Larry King Live,* one of Simpson's attorneys was asked whether O. J. bought a not-guilty verdict. His response: "O. J. didn't buy justice; every defendant deserves the kind of defense O. J. was able to afford." Perhaps he was right. If you or someone you cared about was accused of murder, you would surely want a defense team as skillful and thorough as O. J.'s. Of course, the critical point is that almost no other person charged with murder can afford the kind of defense Mr. Simpson was able to buy. Although in principle every defendant has broad constitutional rights, in practice, full use of those rights costs money—lots of it. And money is something defendants in murder trials have very little of. As Justice William O. Douglas observed, "One searches our chronicles in vain for the execution of any member of the affluent strata of this society."

As a contrast, consider the case of Ernest Dwayne Jones. His trial took place down the hall from Simpson's. Mr. Jones stood accused of raping and viciously stabbing to death Julia Miller, his girlfriend's mother. Her body was found with two kitchen knives sticking out of her neck. There were no eyewitnesses. Jones was mentally disturbed, had a history of being sexually abused, and had grown up with two alcoholic parents. He also had a previous history of violence. Ten years prior, he had been convicted of rape and he had served six years in prison.

In Jones's trial there was one public defender and one prosecutor. The prosecution's DNA evidence, which was analyzed by the same company used in the Simpson case, was presented in a day. Unlike the Simpson trial, there were no renowned defense experts to raise suspicions about contamination or bias in the laboratory analysis. There was no defense attorney with special expertise in DNA evidence to grill the prosecution expert. In fact, in the Jones trial, the DNA expert was not even cross-examined by the defender. The trial lasted twelve days and Jones was found guilty. It took another four days to complete the penalty phase and sentence Mr. Jones to death. When asked to compare the two trials, the foreman of the Jones jury said, "If they brought in other experts and overwhelmed us with clever data and impressive people, they might at least have got the jury to hang." He added that "if [Jones] had gotten Johnnie Cochran and his resources, he wouldn't be sentenced to death."[131] But Jones couldn't afford the team of lawyers that might have saved his life.

Or consider the case of Demetrie Mayfield, who was tried not in Los Angeles County but in neighboring San Bernadino County. His case was even more similar to Simpson's. Mayfield was accused of murdering a woman friend and a man who (like Ronald Goldman) was apparently in the wrong place at the wrong time. Mayfield's attorney spent a total of forty hours preparing for the trial. His only real interview with the defendant took place the morning before the trial began. Mayfield now lives on death row.[132]

Imagine that you have been charged with capital murder. Perhaps it was a case of mistaken identity, perhaps you had to kill in self-defense, maybe someone you were with pulled the trigger. You would want a swift, thorough investigation of the crime, you would want all potential witnesses interviewed, you would want experts to sift painstakingly through the physical evidence, you would want to hire a jury-selection expert, you would want to hire your own experts to contradict the prosecution's experts. Most of all, you would want the best, most experienced defense attorney you could find. The lawyer is crucial. Your lawyer will prepare the case, prepare the witnesses, file motions, cross-examine witnesses, explain slippery concepts (like premeditation, aggravation, and mitigation) to the jury, object to improper questions by the prosecution, fight to get favorable evidence admitted and to get unfavorable evidence excluded. All of these services are available to every American—for a price. If the price is more than you can afford, you are entitled to a court-appointed attorney. But not necessarily a good or experienced attorney. Maybe you'll get lucky and wind up with a good attorney. But would you be willing to bet your life on it?

The sad, shameful fact is that money makes the difference between life and death for many defendants. Far too often, it is not those who commit the most despicable crimes who are sent to death row, but those who lack the money to mount an adequate defense. Money can buy a thorough investigation of the crime, expert analysis and testimony, a careful search for mitigating factors that may need to be presented during a penalty phase. Most important, money can buy a skillful, experienced lawyer. Rich people can afford to select their lawyers, but poor people are at the mercy of the attorney assigned to them.

Because very few capital defendants can afford to hire their own lawyer, they are represented by either a public defender or a court-appointed private attorney. Public defenders work for state-funded offices that specialize in representing indigent clients. Fortunately, there are many dedicated public defenders who are both capable and experienced in defending people accused of capital crimes, and these defenders manage to provide effective representation despite relatively low pay and heavy workloads. But there are not nearly enough to go around. Most public defenders' offices are located in large cities and many states have no such office. In these states, capital defendants are represented by court-appointed lawyers: private attorneys assigned by trial judges.

The effectiveness of defense attorneys in capital cases varies wildly. Most states have a cap on spending for each capital trial. For example, Alabama pays attorneys at the rate of $20 per hour, and Mississippi pays only $11.75 per hour.[133] Stephen Bright, a lawyer who has defended many capital defendants, reports that his pay for representing a capital defendant in Mississippi amounted to less than $2 per hour. He notes that in many capital cases, "the court reporter is paid more than the lawyer appointed to defend the accused."[134] Because of unrealistic limits on the total amount of money the state allocates for the defense of a capital client, the available funds are often exhausted before the trial even begins. Appallingly, capital defendants with court-appointed lawyers are more than twice as likely to be sentenced to death than defendants with privately retained attorneys.[135]

In most cases the balance of resources between defense and prosecution is not equal. Like public defenders, prosecutors tend to carry a heavy caseload. But they tend to be better paid and they have considerably more resources at their disposal. Typically, defenders must file motions to fund investigations, to obtain laboratory analysis of physical evidence, to hire psychologists or jury experts or expert witnesses. In contrast, prosecutors are able to use the local police forces as their investigative teams, and they have access to crime labs and pathologists from the coroner's office. While court-appointed lawyers are often inexperienced and unfamiliar with relevant law, prosecutors' offices are staffed with experienced attorneys, and even novice prosecutors have ready access to the expertise of more seasoned colleagues. Outside of public defenders' offices, there is no comparable network for defenders in capital trials.

In Alabama, Judy Haney was charged with killing her husband. Midway through the trial, her court-appointed attorney was held in contempt for coming to court drunk. The attorney spent the night in jail but proceeded to act as her lawyer when the trial resumed the next morning. A few days later, Haney was convicted and sentenced to death. Her careless lawyer had neglected to present crucial mitigating evidence that the dead husband had abused Haney and her children for nearly fifteen years. Despite the considerable failings of her attorney, the conviction and the death sentence were upheld by the Alabama Supreme Court.

In Texas, Jesus Romero was executed in 1992. His sentence had been upheld even though he had received a woefully inadequate defense. Here is the entire penalty-phase argument of his court-appointed lawyer: "You are an extremely intelligent jury. You've got that man's life in your hands. You can take it or not. That's all I have to say."[136] This is hardly the impassioned, eloquent appeal we would hope for when a defendant's life is at stake. It appears that other attorneys are nearly as terse. For example, in Louisiana, capital trials last an average of three days and penalty phases last an average of 2.9 hours.[137]

John Young was executed in 1985 in Georgia. Not long after Young's trial, his defense lawyer was sent to prison for state and federal narcotics convictions. The attorney later submitted an affidavit to the appeals court confessing that he had spent "hardly any time preparing for the case" and had been unable to concentrate on the case because of "a myriad of personal problems."[138] The repentant attorney went on to say that he had failed to investigate the life of the defendant in search of mitigating evidence. This was unfortunate, because an investigation would have revealed a tragic story. At the age of three, the defendant had witnessed the murder of his mother while he was lying in bed with her. He was raised by an alcoholic relative who allowed him to become involved in child prostitution and drug abuse. Such information would not have affected the guilt phase of the trial, but it might have moved a jury to sentence Young to life in prison. As Justice Thurgood Marshall observed, many defense attorneys

> are handling their first criminal cases, or their first murder cases, when confronted with the prospect of a death penalty. Though acting in good faith, they inevitably make very serious mistakes. . . . Counsel have been unaware that . . . claims should be preserved; that certain findings by a jury might preclude imposition of the death penalty; or that a separate sentencing phase will follow a conviction. The federal courts are filled with stories of counsel who presented

no evidence in mitigation of their client's sentence because they did not know what to offer or how to offer it, or had not read the state's sentencing statute.[139]

Advocates of the death penalty might argue that most errors resulting from deficient lawyering are remedied on appeal. But a sloppy, cursory defense at trial has lasting effects on the defendant's prospects on appeal. Clearly, the appeals process does correct some errors. But the process is far from perfect. There are significant legal barriers to making an appeal based on issues that were not raised in the initial trial. To preserve a claim for later appeal, an attorney must often raise the relevant issue (e.g., admission of improper evidence, failure to admit crucial evidence, composition of the jury) during the initial trial. Otherwise, the defendant may forfeit the right to have the claim considered on appeal. Furthermore, the defendant must show that the lawyer's mistakes were serious enough to violate the constitutional right to "effective assistance of counsel." Recent Supreme Court decisions make it necessary for appellate lawyers to prove that the errors were consequential enough to change the outcome of the case.

Charles Black Jr. has argued that our system of capital punishment is "saturated with discretion." He describes the criminal justice system as a long series of decisions: to arrest or not, to charge or not, to plea-bargain or to go to trial, to seek the death penalty or not, to convict or acquit, to sentence to life in prison or death by execution, on what grounds to appeal, and whether to pardon or commute a sentence of death. He makes the point forcefully:

Can you really doubt that a process like this, from first to last, is heavily loaded against the poor? Could you really be surprised at the finding that by far the majority of people suffering death are poor? Are you satisfied with that? If you are not, face the fact that there is no way to change it except to do away with the death penalty.[140]

Justice in Black and White

During the time of slavery there was no pretense of equal justice. Slaves were regarded as property and slave owners could abuse their property in most any way they saw fit. The so-called Black Codes stipulated in law that blacks could be treated far more severely than whites for similar crimes. Prior to the Civil War in the South, blacks could be put to death for a variety of crimes. The rape of a black woman was not considered a crime, but many black men were killed for the alleged rape of a white woman. Blacks could be executed for property crimes such as burglary or arson, while whites were permitted to pay a fine or serve a short jail term. Blacks faced not only harsher punishments but also formidable procedural obstacles: They could not testify in court against whites, and they could not serve on juries.

Unofficial "justice" could be even harsher than that dispensed by the official courts. Recorded lynchings numbered 1,540 during the 1890s, and another 1,951 lynchings took place between 1900 and the end of the 1930s. The yearly number of lynchings often exceeded the number of official executions, and black men were overwhelmingly the targets of these spontaneous killings.[141] At the turn of the century, one commentator summarized the prevailing view of such punishments:

The frequent atrocity of the crimes committed by negroes of low character, without apparently any particular provocation, is something scarcely to be understood—the adjectives wanton, bestial, outrageous, brutal and inhuman all seem wholly inadequate to express the feeling of utter disgust and abhorrence that is aroused. . . . Southern whites have found the law and its administration utterly unsuited to the function of dealing with negro criminals—hence, the frequent adoption of summary and extra-legal methods of punishment.[142]

Lynchings of black men for the alleged rape of white women were so frequent that in newspaper accounts of the time it was simply reported that a negro man was hanged for "the usual crime." Even in more modern times, blacks have been disproportionately sentenced to death for the crime of rape. An especially thorough investigation by Marvin Wolfgang and Marc Riedel examined 361 rape convictions during the period 1945 to 1965.[143] After controlling for a variety of variables, they found that the best predictor of a death sentence was the race of the offender combined with the race of the victim. Black men convicted of raping white women were the group most likely to be sentenced to death by a shocking margin. Four hundred and fifty-five men were executed for rape between 1930 and 1967 and 89 percent of those men were black. In *Coker v. Georgia* (1977), the Supreme Court ended the death penalty for rape in cases where the victim was not killed.

But that was all a long time ago. Now both blacks and whites are subject to the same laws and members of both groups are routinely sentenced to death for capital murders. Yet there is still a disturbing imbalance. Here are some statistics: At present, the U.S. population is about 12 percent black but the population of death row is 41 percent black;[144] since the reinstatement of the death penalty in 1976, 39.3 percent of the people killed in the execution chamber have been black, and 86 percent of the executions have been people convicted of killing whites, even though roughly half of all murder victims in the United States are black.[145] There have been more than 16,000 executions in American jurisdictions since 1608, yet only 31 whites have been executed for killing a black person. Perhaps such statistics are misleading or inconclusive, but even the most ardent supporters of capital punishment would concede that these striking disparities should make us suspicious.

More important is the pattern of sentencing since the 1976 restructuring of the capital trial. Maybe the problems have been fixed. Unfortunately, the evidence suggests that, despite three decades of legal and procedural tinkering, the death penalty remains capricious, flawed, and discriminatory. Just prior to his retirement in 1994, Justice Harry Blackmun, who had formerly supported capital punishment, concluded that "race continues to play a major role in determining who shall live and who shall die."

Racial bias seeps into the decision-making process at every juncture. It is not primarily the race of the defendant that influences decisions, but the race of the victim. William Bowers and Glenn Pierce looked at 700 homicides and found that offenders whose victims were white were more than twice as likely to be indicted for first-degree murder than offenders whose victims were black. In an examination of over 600 murders, Michael Radelet found that while overall 70 percent of homicides led to first-degree murder indictments, over 92 percent of black offender—white victim murders led to first-degree indictments.[146]

A similar pattern emerges when we examine the decision of whether or not to seek the death penalty. Research indicates that if the victim is white, prosecutors are more than twice as likely to seek a death sentence than if the victim is black, and blacks who kill whites are almost four times as likely to be charged with capital murder than blacks who kill blacks.[147] A study that looked at over 700 murders in New Jersey during the 1980s found that the decision to seek a death sentence was strongly influenced by race of the victim. Prosecutors decided to seek a death sentence for 43 percent of the white-victim murders but only for 28 percent of the black-victim murders. When researchers looked at the race of both victim and offender in combination, they found that prosecutors sought the death penalty in just over half of the black killer–white victim cases, but in only 20 percent of the white killer–black victim cases.[148] In the most sophisticated analysis of the issue, David Baldus, George Woodworth, and Charles Pulaski found that, even after taking over twenty relevant variables into account, prosecutors decided to seek the death penalty five times more often against killers of whites than against killers of blacks.[149]

Only about a quarter of the defendants convicted of capital murder are sentenced to death (although there is tremendous variability from state to state). It is not entirely clear why the other three-quarters are spared. An optimistic inference might be that juries and judges are properly weighing legally relevant criteria and sending only the worst, most barbarous criminals to the execution chamber. There is some evidence to support this inference; several studies have found that the probability of a death sentence is increased when there is more than one victim, when there is another violent felony (e.g., rape), when the victim was a stranger to the offender, and when the murder was especially brutal.[150] Clearly, these are important factors that ought to be considered when making the life-or-death decision. But these are not the only factors that are considered.

Decisions about whether to charge and whether to seek the death penalty occur before the trial begins. It would be comforting to think that the biases that infect those early decisions are somehow corrected during the later stages, during the guilt and penalty trials. Unfortunately, the research shows that later stages only amplify the bias. In a large-scale study of capital sentencing in four states, William Bowers and Glenn Pierce compared the sentences of blacks who killed whites with the sentences of blacks who killed blacks in Ohio, Florida, Georgia, and Texas. In Ohio, the black offender–white victim group was 15 times more likely to receive a death sentence, in Florida they were 37 times more likely, in Georgia they were 33 times more likely, and in Texas they were 87 times more likely.[151] Data from other states led to similar conclusions. For example, even after taking the characteristics of the crime into account, Gross and Mauro found that killing a white person increased the odds of being sentenced to death by a factor of 4 in Illinois, a factor of 7 in Georgia, and a factor of nearly 5 in Florida.[152]

A particularly interesting and consistent finding is that racial bias vanishes when the murder is especially brutal and the defendant has a history of violent crimes. When judging the worst murders, race (of the defendant or of the victim) doesn't seem to matter.[153] Racial bias only creeps in when aggravation is relatively weak and the choice between life and death is difficult. This may be how race finds its way into our system of capital punishment. While some murders are so vicious and violent that race doesn't matter, in less brutal murders both prosecutors and jurors may unintentionally let race influence their decision-making processes. For example, although seldom discussed openly, part of the calculation in deciding whether to try for the death penalty has to do with what some prosecutors call "victim quality." The reasoning is that jurors are more likely to impose a sentence of death if the victim is easy to admire or identify with. It is easier to obtain a death sentence if the victim was a hardworking young mother than if the victim was a drug addict with a long arrest record. It is even possible that the decision not to seek the death penalty is simply a pragmatic calculation made by prosecutors who (correctly) believe that when aggravation is low or moderate, it will be more difficult to obtain a death sentence if the victim was black.

Victim quality is not on any official list of aggravating factors. But jurors, perhaps unconsciously, assess the worth of the victim. Jurors may simply find it easier to identify with victims who are similar to them. Because most jurors in the United States are white, they may find it harder to empathize with black victims. It is also possible that the murder of a white person may subjectively seem more frightening and personally threatening to jurors. If the killer is black and the victim is white, it may have an especially strong impact on white jurors. In those cases where the argument for sending someone to the execution chamber is not overwhelming, similarity between jurors and the victim may come into play, and in some cases it may become the decisive factor.

Racial bias may be *especially* likely in capital cases because they arouse such strong emotions. A dispassionate, rational analysis is exceedingly difficult when confronted with a hideous crime. Also, the concepts that lie at the very heart of the penalty decision (e.g., aggravation and mitigation) are quite slippery. Because the decision must go beyond a mere mechanical weighing of facts, there is plenty of room for bias and prejudice to seep into the process. While racial and other forms of prejudice may exert little influence on factual determinations—understanding the angle of a stab wound or the trajectory of a bullet—the question of whether a defendant should live or die is infused with subjectivity. The complex, value-laden issue of who deserves to die is susceptible to subtle and even unconscious bias.

Several conclusions can be drawn from the research on racial disparities in capital cases: Those who are accused of murdering a white victim are more likely to be charged with a capital crime; those convicted of killing a white victim are more likely to receive a sentence of death; black defendants who are convicted of killing a white person are the group most likely to receive the death penalty; white defendants who murder black victims are the group least likely to receive a death sentence; and the effects of race are most pronounced in southern states like Texas, Georgia, Louisiana, and Florida.[154]

The Supreme Court's View of Race

In 1987 the United States Supreme Court heard evidence about racial discrimination in the case of *McCleskey v. Kemp*. Warren McCleskey had been sentenced to death for killing a police officer during the robbery of a furniture store. A major basis for his appeal to the Supreme Court was the claim that his death sentence was a result of discrimination: He was black and his victim was white. McCleskey had compelling evidence in his favor: an exceedingly thorough and statistically sophisticated study of charging and sentencing in Georgia over a six-year period. The study, which examined the effect of race on capital sentencing practices, was conducted by David Baldus, George Woodworth, and Charles Pulaski.

Baldus and his colleagues analyzed 594 homicides in Georgia. They found that blacks convicted of killing whites were sentenced to death in 22 percent of capital cases, whereas whites convicted of killing blacks received a death sentence only 3 percent of the time. The researchers then looked at the 594 homicides, taking into account over 250 characteristics of the crime, the offender, and the victim. A major finding was that, after controlling for a host of legally relevant variables, the odds of receiving a death sentence were 4.3 times higher for murderers of whites than for murderers of blacks.[155] Based on these findings, attorneys for McCleskey argued that the racially discriminatory pattern of sentencing violated his constitutional right to equal protection under the law.

A majority of the justices were unpersuaded by the evidence. In a sharply divided 5-to-4 decision, the high Court ruled that the striking pattern of racially discriminatory death sentencing did not show that McCleskey's constitutional right to equal protection had been violated. Writing for the majority, Justice Powell asserted that a successful challenge would need to prove intentional discrimination against a particular defendant. The defense would need to present "evidence specific to his own case that would support an inference that racial consideration played a part in his sentence."[156] The Court further held that some lack of fairness was tolerable and inevitable because discretion is an essential component of any capital sentencing scheme.

Given the reasoning offered for rejecting the claim of discrimination in *McCleskey*, it is difficult to imagine a case of racial discrimination that the current Supreme Court would find compelling. At least for now, the *McCleskey* decision has made it virtually impossible to demonstrate that our system of death sentencing is unconstitutional because it discriminates on the basis of race. Patterns of sentencing had been examined over a period of years, taking into consideration virtually every relevant case characteristic that could be measured. Perhaps a particular defendant could win a claim based on racial discrimination, but he or she would need to prove that the discrimination was intentional. That would be very difficult. Even when intentional racial bias influences the sentencing decision, it is rare for the decision-makers to confess that they willfully discriminated against a defendant.

Although a majority of Supreme Court justices seem undisturbed by the way death sentences are handed down, lawyers working on the front lines appear to have serious reservations. In 1997 the American Bar Association called for a moratorium on executions until the inequities of the current system can be fixed. The ABA is the largest legal organization in the United States, with a membership including both defense and prosecuting attorneys. Citing "a haphazard maze of unfair practices," the ABA's House of Delegates voted to halt executions by greater than a 2-to-1 margin.[157] In denouncing the current system, the ABA made note of racial discrimination in the imposition of the penalty, the shortage of competent defense attorneys in capital cases, the lack of fair compensation for defense attorneys, the weakening of federal *habeas* reviews, and the growing risk of executing innocent people.

Wrongful Conviction and Execution

Many condemned prisoners go to the execution chamber proclaiming their innocence. Some are telling the truth.

No one thinks our criminal justice system is infallible. The criticism heard most often is that judges and juries are too soft, and that sometimes real criminals go free or serve short sentences. Clearly there is truth in this charge. Still, we must not close our eyes to the reality of error in the opposite direction, the reality that sometimes the system wrongfully arrests, convicts, imprisons, and occasionally even executes an innocent person. This is the most troubling form of error in capital cases. Although some might claim that mistakes don't occur, this is not a serious argument. No reasonable person genuinely believes that our system is so perfectly constructed and calibrated that such mistakes never happen. However, since some reasonable people do seem to believe that such errors are a thing of the past, here are a few recent examples:

• In 1996, Rolando Cruz was allowed to walk out of his death-row cell after eleven long years. He had been convicted of the rape and murder of a ten-year-old Chicago girl. No physical evidence had ever linked Cruz to the crime, and no motive was ever established. Lacking real evidence, the police created phony evidence. They claimed that during interrogation, Cruz had recounted a "dream" that contained specific details about the killing—details only the real killer could have known. Prosecutors disclosed the "dream" evidence only four days before the trial. Although most of the interrogation was tape-recorded, the portion describing the "dream" sequence was not.[158] Even though the man who had actually committed the murder had confessed to the crime eight years earlier, it took a new DNA test to exonerate Cruz.

• In 1993, Walter McMillian was released from Alabama's death row when the state admitted to withholding evidence that the key eyewitness had lied. "It's a horrible feeling," said McMillian. "I had a lot of faith that I wouldn't be [killed], but still, I knew it was a possibility".[159] In the same year, Kirk

Bloodsworth was released from death row when DNA testing proved that he did not commit the murder for which he was sentenced to die.

• On May 12, 1993, Leonel Torres Herrera was executed in Texas. He had been convicted of killing two police officers. During the decade he waited on death row, four witnesses filed affidavits saying that it was Herrera's brother (who had since died) who had fired the shots that killed the officers. The son of the now dead brother, who was hiding in the room when the shooting occurred, swore that he had seen his father shoot the police officers. Two other witnesses swore that the brother had confessed to committing the murders. The United States Supreme Court was not convinced, and Herrera was put to death.[160]

• In 1995, a mildly retarded man with an IQ of about 65 was set free by order of the governor of Missouri. Johnny Lee Wilson, a janitor at a local school, was convicted of the brutal murder of a seventy-nine-year-old woman whose bound, beaten body was found in her home. Wilson's confession had come after several hours of intense interrogation by investigators. His "confession" contained only the facts provided to him by his interrogators. But he spent more than eight years in prison before his name was cleared.[161]

• In 1995, Jesse Dewayne Jacobs was killed in a Texas execution chamber. He had been convicted of shooting and killing the ex-wife of his sister's boyfriend. The conviction seemed unassailable. After all, Jacobs had confessed to the murder. The problem came when Jacobs recanted after the trial, now claiming that his sister had pulled the trigger. Surprisingly, the sister was later convicted of involuntary manslaughter for the shooting. The prosecutor who won that conviction said publicly that he doubted Jacobs's guilt. But in Jacobs's final appeal, the United States Supreme Court denied a stay of execution in a 6-to-3 decision. Writing for the minority, John Paul Stevens said, "I find this course of events deeply troubling."[162]

The list of wrongful convictions for murder could fill the remainder of this book. But it is more important to look for the underlying causes of these tragic mistakes. By far the best work in this area has been done over a period of three decades by Hugo Bedau of Tufts University and Michael Radelet of the University of Florida. They identified 416 people who were wrongfully convicted of murder and sentenced to death between 1900 and the summer of 1991. All of these people were imprisoned. Over 30 of them came within days or minutes of being executed. In 23 cases, the innocent person was executed. Bedau and Radelet continue to uncover such errors at the rate of about a dozen per year.[163]

It is likely that these figures vastly underestimate the incidence of "wrong person" errors. It is impossible to know how many erroneous convictions are never remedied. Although a condemned prisoner may claim that he is innocent, he is in no position to prove it. Proving innocence and getting the courts to listen to new evidence is almost always the result of the tireless efforts of family members, defense lawyers, or journalists. These efforts must yield results *before* the prisoner is led to the execution chamber. The incentive for further investigation goes to the grave with the executed prisoner, and the case is usually closed with the coffin. Once the defendant has been killed, defense attorneys, investigators, and journalists turn their attention to other cases, cases where the defendant is still alive. Better to spend limited time and money on those defendants who still might be rescued before their date with the executioner. Add to this the deep reluctance of officials to admit serious error, and it becomes clear why the execution of innocent people is severely underestimated.

What makes wrongful convictions especially disturbing is that most are caused by factors that are not detected by legal review. The four main sources of error are police error (coerced or false confession, sloppy or corrupt investigation), prosecutor error (suppression of exculpatory evidence, overzealousness), witness error (mistaken eyewitness identification, perjured testimony), and a variety of other errors that don't fit into any neat category. These miscellaneous errors include misleading circumstantial evidence, forensic science errors, incompetent defense lawyers, exculpatory evidence ruled inadmissible, inadequate attention to alibis, and pressure created by community outrage. The most common means of discovering these devastating mistakes are confession by the actual perpetrator, evidence uncovered through the perseverance of a dedicated defense counsel, and the publicity generated by concerned members of the media.[164]

Some say that we must reluctantly accept such errors as the unfortunate price for the unique benefits of executions. If the death penalty has extraordinary advantages as compared to its alternatives, perhaps it is reasonable to accept the discrimination, arbitrariness, and error that have always infected the application of capital punishment. But are there extraordinary advantages? When evaluating the benefits of any policy, there is always an implicit comparison: Beneficial as compared to what? The usual alternative to the death penalty is life imprisonment without the possibility of parole. This alternative punishment not only satisfies our goal of protecting society, it also eliminates the risk of killing innocent people or threatening them with execution.

Beyond the well-documented evidence that mistakes continue to accumulate, there is no rational basis for believing that innocent people have become better protected against wrongful executions in recent years. A few legal scholars have suggested a series of reforms that would help to reduce (but not eliminate) "wrong person" errors. However, there has been almost no effort to adopt these well-considered but expensive and time-consuming reforms.[165] As discussed earlier, the only major procedural reforms in capital cases were the result of the *Gregg v. Georgia* decision of 1976. These reforms, which included introduction of the two-phase trial and automatic appeals in capital cases, did not directly address what we now know to be the major sources of error in capital cases: suppressed or fabricated evidence, mistaken eyewitness identification, shoddy investigation, and incompetent lawyering.

To make things worse, judges and politicians are now acting in ways that are likely to *increase* the probability of mistakes. Scores of politicians have attacked the appeals process in capital cases, referring to it as "endless," "frivolous," "interminable," and "excessive." These attacks come at a time when the quality of the appeals process has been significantly compromised. For example, the California Supreme Court now affirms more than 96 percent of the capital cases it reviews.[166] In a move that will further weaken the ability of defendants to appeal convictions or sentences, Congress voted in 1995 to cut off funds to more than twenty centers that provide legal assistance for death-row inmates who are pursuing appeals.[169] And in 1996, the federal "anti-terrorism" bill limited capital defendants to a single federal appeal. The trend is not to scrutinize cases more carefully, but to move them through the system more quickly. The slow road to the execution chamber is being replaced by a superhighway.

Why Death Is Different

When confronted with evidence that the death penalty discriminates against those with dark skin and empty wallets and that occasionally innocent people are convicted, imprisoned, or executed, some reply that although mistakes are regrettable, some degree of error must be always be tolerated. No system will ever be perfect. The problem with this argument—as philosophers, jurists, and religious leaders have pointed out for decades—is that "death is different." That is, killing a prisoner is qualitatively different from any other form of punishment. Just as paying a fine is different from serving a prison term, death is different from confinement.

But what makes death unique? First, execution is the most severe form of punishment permitted in our system of justice (slow torture was long ago deemed unworthy of a civilized society). Not only is killing an extreme form of punishment, but the preliminaries are also terrifying. Condemned prisoners wait in their cells for a period of years, contemplating their fate. As appeals fail, their already-meager hope evaporates, and the prisoner knows that someday a team of guards will escort him down the cellblock, prepare him to be killed, and crank up the machinery that will end his life.

Second, the punishment of death is irrevocable. Once the prisoner has been killed, there is no possibility of reversing an error. An imprisoned man who is later found to be innocent can be released, but a corpse cannot be brought back to life. If a man is wrongly imprisoned, no amount of money can compensate him for the part of his life that has been lost, but at least he can try to enjoy what remains of his life. After an execution, it is simply too late. Even if the truth is discovered before his appointment with the executioner, the condemned prisoner will still have suffered the psychological torture of anticipating his own approaching death. Because killing is a uniquely severe and final punishment, we must demand a higher standard of certainty and consistency. The harsher the punishment, the greater the need for certainty. If you receive a ticket because of a faulty parking meter, you have been treated unjustly. Still, your loss is not great. A small amount of error is tolerable. If you are wrongly imprisoned for ten years, your loss is far greater. If you are wrongly killed for a crime you did not commit, the loss is intolerable. As long as we kill as a form of punishment, such intolerable errors are inevitable.

Killing, if it is permitted at all, is a penalty that ought to be reserved for the most egregious crimes. Wealth and race should not be part of the calculation. But money and color have always influenced decisions about who should be sent to the execution chamber and who should be sent to prison. It is unrealistic to think that we can ever cleanse our death-penalty system of such pernicious influences. Even if we could, we would still occasionally convict, sentence, and execute innocent people.

The only true solution to these problems is to abolish the penalty.

CHAPTER SIX

Does the Death Penalty Deter Potential Murderers?

Fear is the mother of safety.

—Sir Francis Bacon

Murder and capital punishment are not opposites that cancel one another out but similars that breed their kind.

—George Bernard Shaw

The theory is simple and self-evident: Fear of the execution chamber will restrain potential murderers. Knowing that they could face the executioner, those who would otherwise kill will stop short of killing. Innocent lives will be saved.

The theory is called deterrence. It has served as a compelling justification for the death penalty since ancient times. The idea is appealing because it is an elaboration of what we know to be true in our own lives: If the potential punishment for a particular behavior is great, we are likely to avoid that behavior. For example, if you work downtown where parking spaces are scarce, you may occasionally risk a $20 or $30 fine for parking illegally. But if the fine is raised to $1,000, only the wealthy will be undeterred. Common sense tells us that the death penalty deters. But common sense also tells us that the earth stands still and the sun moves across the sky. Only after looking at the evidence do we become convinced that we walk on a spinning planet that slowly circles the sun.

As capital punishment became morally troubling to many Americans, the justification of deterrence gained prominence. It offered a seemingly scientific rationale for executions. Supporters of capital punishment were not out for primitive revenge, they were simply discouraging future murders and thereby protecting the public. Quotes from scripture were bolstered by appeals to reason. Even today, for those who favor dispassionate cost-benefit analyses, deterrence provides a coolly logical basis for favoring executions.

For well over a century researchers have been investigating whether or not the death penalty serves as a deterrent. There are now over 200 studies on the topic. The theory of deterrence implies a couple of hypotheses that can be tested by looking closely at murder rates. The first hypothesis is that places with capital punishment should have lower murder rates than places where execution is not an available sanction. The fear created in the hearts and minds of potential murderers should suppress their homicidal impulses. If, for example, one state has the death penalty and another state does not, the death-penalty state should have proportionately fewer killings. This hypothesis has been thoroughly tested.

The Evidence

One of the earliest studies was conducted by a Massachusetts legislator named Robert Rantoul. In the 1840s, Rantoul compiled statistics on murder and execution rates in several nations over a forty-year period. In 1846 he presented his findings: The deterrent effect was illusory. Indeed, his data revealed a counter-deterrence effect: "Murders have rapidly diminished in those countries in which executions are scarcely known; slightly in France where the change of policy was not so great; while in England, . . . under a milder administration of the law, there has been a change for the better."[168] Since Rantoul's time, hundreds of studies have been conducted to assess the deterrent power of capital punishment. Nearly all of them lend credence to Rantoul's early conclusions.

Critics of this early research countered that the United States is different from other countries. What failed to work in Europe may be effective here. And indeed, the United States furnishes a splendid laboratory for putting deterrence theory to the test. Some states have the death penalty, other states do not. Some states have adopted the death penalty, only to abandon it later. Some states have even adopted the death penalty, abolished it later, only to reinstate it even later. These differences between states enable researchers to conduct multiple tests of the theory. Specifically, the theory predicts that states with capital punishment will have lower murder rates than states without capital punishment. Of course it's a bit more complicated than that, because the states being compared must be as similar as possible. Comparing Oregon, Florida, and Delaware might not be especially informative because these three states differ on several important dimensions. A better test—the test used in the research literature—uses geographically adjacent states, states that tend to share many features including history, culture, and economy. In the 1960s, a sociologist named Thorsten Sellin made just such comparisons. Supporters of capital punishment found no comfort in his findings.

Sellin examined clusters of states that were similar in most respects. He found, for example, that North Dakota, a state without the death penalty, had a lower homicide rate than two similar states that did have the death penalty, South Dakota and Nebraska. Michigan, a non-capital punishment state, had an identical murder rate to Indiana, and a lower rate than Ohio, both of which had the death penalty. Rhode Island, a state that only carried the penalty of life imprisonment, was compared to two death-penalty states, Massachusetts and Connecticut. Rhode Island's murder rate was lower than Connecticut's and identical to Massachusetts's. To be sure, a couple of states without the death penalty (e.g., Maine) had higher rates than comparable states with the death penalty (e.g., New Hampshire). But overall, the states with execution chambers had rates of murder that were significantly higher than states that did not execute murderers.[169]

But maybe things have changed. After all, Sellin's data examined the years 1920 to 1955. It is possible that changes in American culture or the legal system—especially modifications in the trial process since the *Furman* and *Gregg* decisions—have made the deterrent effect more powerful. Several researchers set out to see if deterrence had changed with the times. Ruth Peterson and William Bailey examined homicide rates for a twelve-year period spanning from 1973 to 1984. Comparing similar, adjacent states, they found that the annual murder rate in states with the death penalty was higher than in states that had abolished it. Specifically, the average murder rate in states with the death penalty was 8.64 for every 100,000 people. In states without the death penalty, the rate was 5.35.[170]

Deterrence theory makes other predictions. A second testable hypothesis has to do with the effects, over time, of getting rid of or bringing back the death penalty. If the death penalty is abandoned in a particular state, murder rates should climb because the fear of execution has been removed. Conversely, if a particular place establishes the death penalty or restores it after a long period of absence, then murder rates should fall. The studies described above included this kind of longitudinal analysis of homicide rates when the death penalty was in effect and when it was suspended for a period of years. These analyses revealed no deterrence effect.

In 1983, Richard Lempert looked for a relationship between the number of executions and number of homicides. He included several states over a fifteen-year period. No relationship was found. His conclusion echoed that of earlier researchers: "The death penalty in general and executions in particular do not deter homicide."[171] The conclusions of studies conducted in the United States were confirmed in research conducted abroad. Dane Archer and Rosemary Gartner measured the murder rate in twelve countries and two foreign cities before and after abolition of the death penalty. Eight of the fourteen cases (57 percent) showed a decreased murder rate in the year following abolition, while only five (36 percent) showed an increase. Further, when they examined longer periods of time, there was even less support for the deterrence hypothesis.[172] When looking at this research, it is essential to keep in mind that there are two fundamental public-policy questions: Will abolishing the death penalty increase the murder rate? and, Will reinstating the death penalty cause the murder rate to drop? Based on the research, the answer to both questions is clearly no.

But maybe comparisons between death-penalty states and non–death penalty states are inconclusive. Maybe the paired states were different in a variety of unnoticed and unmeasured ways. Maybe even adjacent states aren't similar enough and researchers were comparing apples and oranges. This basic criticism spawned a new wave of deterrence research. This new wave looked at the effect of the death penalty over long periods of time, and used complex statistical procedures to control for or remove the impact of factors that might influence the number of murders. By taking into account several factors that were known to contribute to murder rates, researchers hoped to purify their comparisons.

One of the first studies to make use of such sophisticated statistical controls was conducted by Baldus and Cole in 1975.[173] Like earlier researchers, they looked at contiguous states. But unlike earlier researchers, they took into account several characteristics known to influence murder rates: unemployment, probability of arrest and conviction, percent of the population between the ages of fifteen and twenty-four, per capita financial expenditures on the police force, and other factors. Even after controlling for all of these factors, no deterrent effect was found. After scores of studies and decades of data analysis, few people found any reason to believe in deterrence. Things looked bleak for deterrence theorists. Then, in 1975, an economist named Isaac Ehrlich came to their rescue.

Ehrlich argued that most of the previous research failed to consider important differences between states. Using a sophisticated statistical technique called multiple regression, he looked at the impact of the death penalty on murder in the United States from 1933 to 1969. Taking into account arrest and conviction rate, unemployment rate, per capita income, population between the ages of fourteen and twenty-four, and other variables, Ehrlich examined what he called "execution risk." This risk was defined as the ratio of executions to convictions for murder. After churning through the data, Ehrlich declared that he had uncovered a powerful deterrent effect.[174]

Ehrlich's findings found an enthusiastic audience. Politicians and policy-makers who supported the death penalty were eager to embrace any research that reinforced their position. And, at the time, Ehrlich's was the only apparently credible study that had managed to detect any deterrent effect. Even better, Ehrlich's findings could be expressed as a pithy slogan: "Every execution prevents seven or eight murders." This lone study supporting a deterrent effect was also cited in the *Gregg v. Georgia* decision of 1976. Balancing the Ehrlich study against the scores of studies that found no deterrent effect, the Supreme Court concluded that "statistical attempts to evaluate the worth of the death penalty as a deterrent to crime by potential offenders have . . . simply been inconclusive."[175]

Because of Ehrlich's highly mathematical approach, only other social scientists could discern the flaws in his research. Almost immediately, critiques began to appear in the research literature. A closer look at the data revealed a striking anomaly: When the last few years (1963 to 1969) were removed from the analysis, the impact of "execution risk" was to increase rather than decrease the number of murders. Other critics pointed out that Ehrlich had failed to include several critical factors in his analysis: rural-to-urban migration, gun ownership, level of violent crime, and length of prison sentences. When these and other key factors were taken into account, the deterrent effect evaporated. The fatal blow to Ehrlich's research came from the prestigious National Academy of Sciences. Their panel (headed by a Nobel Prize–winning economist) reanalyzed Ehrlich's data and came to the conclusion that the data showed no deterrent effect.[176]

As the evidence against deterrence continued to accumulate, some people suggested yet another explanation for the absence of a deterrence effect: Researchers were looking at the wrong factors. What mattered was not whether the death penalty was an available sanction, but the number of executions that were actually carried out. Maybe it takes an actual execution to instill fear in the hearts of potential murderers, and it is only this fear that causes them to refrain from killing. And because it is only actual executions that demonstrate the grave consequences of murder, greater publicity should boost the deterrent effect. According to this line of reasoning, sufficient fear will be felt only when an execution is vivid in people's minds—in the days, weeks, and months immediately following an execution. As the memory of each execution fades in the minds of would-be murderers, the deterrent effect might fade and then finally disappear.

This idea that it is only the actual occurrence of an execution (rather than laws authorizing the death penalty) that deters is by no means new. Back in 1935, Robert Dann tabulated the number of murders sixty days before and sixty days after five highly publicized executions. Interestingly, Dann found that the number of murders rose after each execution.[177] More than forty years later (in 1978), King looked at twenty well-publicized executions over more than a decade. His findings also ran contrary to the predictions of deterrence theory: On average, each execution produced an increase of 1.2 homicides.[178] Supporters of deterrence retreated a bit farther and suggested that maybe only well-publicized executions generated the effect. But scores of studies failed to support even this more limited prediction. For example, William Bailey conducted an especially detailed analysis of the impact of television publicity on murder rates in 1990. No effect could be detected. Even when the type of publicity (e.g., graphic versus matter-of-fact coverage) was taken into account, there was no discernable impact on murder rates.[179]

Another issue raised by the defenders of deterrence theory concerned the type of murder for which the death penalty was an available punishment. Many studies of deterrence, especially the older studies, have examined total homicide rates. But not all murders are punishable by death. If we make the dubious assumption that murderers know which types of murders are punishable by death, it is possible that only capital murderers are being deterred. Perhaps the deterrent effect is being masked because noncapital murders are included in the analysis. In response to this criticism, researchers have looked at the murder of police officers. This is a useful measure because killing a police officer is punishable by death in every state that permits capital punishment. Further, it has often been argued that the death penalty is especially useful for deterring fleeing criminals who are in danger of being arrested. Ernest van den Haag, an outspoken supporter of capital punishment, puts it this way:

> Without the death penalty, an offender having committed a crime that leads to imprisonment for life has nothing to lose if he murders the arresting officer. By murdering the officer . . . such criminals increase their chances of escape, without increasing the severity of the punishment they will suffer if caught.[180]

Despite the apparent logic of Van den Haag's argument, there is no evidence that police officers are safer in jurisdictions that have capital punishment. No deterrence of police murders has been found for the time periods 1919 through 1954, 1961 through 1971, or 1973 through 1984. For the two later time periods, the analyses took into account factors such as poverty, race, unemployment, and urbanization.[181]

The most sophisticated investigation of police killings was published by William Bailey and Ruth Peterson in 1994. They looked at police killings for the fourteen years prior to 1990. Their analysis examined several types of police killings (e.g., on-duty versus off-duty) and took into account several key variables: the total number of executions, the number of executions for police killings, the amount of media coverage of such executions, and the type of media attention given to these executions. They even removed the influence of several variables known to be linked to murder rates (i.e., race, number of people living in cities, number of persons aged sixteen to thirty-four, divorce rate, unemployment, and percentage of the population on welfare). Taking into account a host of relevant factors and using a variety of statistical techniques, these researchers were still unable to locate a deterrent effect.[182]

With respect to the death penalty, deterrence theory points in one direction and the facts point in the opposite direction. The fragile logic of deterrence theory has crumbled under the weight of research evidence. More than a century of experience and more than 200 pieces of research lead to an inescapable conclusion: The death penalty does not deter potential murderers. Confronted with the accumulated evidence, people who once made bold claims about the deterrent power of executions have been forced into a long, slow retreat. As each of their arguments was demolished by the facts, deterrence theorists have found new justifications for supporting capital punishment. One keen observer put it this way: "Proponents [of deterrence] increasingly find themselves affirming more idiosyncratic explanations for the effects they presume the death penalty has, but which research has yet to reveal. . . . With each new set of findings their task becomes more arduous and their arguments become less plausible."[183] The burden of proof falls squarely on the shoulders of those who claim to have faith in the power of deterrence. The conclusion that the death penalty does not deter rests on a mountain of evidence built up over several decades. Anyone who manages to detect a deterrent effect must weigh his or her findings against that mountain.

Research on the lack of deterrence will continue to accumulate. And, occasionally, because of a methodological flaw or a statistical anomaly, or an unusual confluence of events, a researcher will trap the elusive deterrent effect. Later, when other researchers look at the same data, the effect will vanish. The supposed deterrent effect of the death penalty looks more and more like some mythical creature whose existence seems less and less probable. There are still people who long to believe in the myth and, for them, no amount of data will dislodge their conviction. Arthur Koestler's words still ring true forty years later: "The defenders of capital punishment are well aware that the statistical evidence is unanswerable. They do not contest it; they ignore it."[184]

Why Killing Doesn't Deter Killers

Perhaps the findings summarized above are unsurprising. After all, the proposition that the death penalty intimidates would-be murderers is based on a thoroughly rational model of human behavior. It assumes that potential killers engage in a dispassionate weighing of the costs and benefits of killing. This assumption is simply wrong. Most murders are crimes of passion—committed under the blinding influence of rage, hatred, jealousy, or fear. To be sure, there are some exceptions, the "hit man" or the terrorist, the calculating husband or wife who kills to collect insurance money. But planned, intentional murders are rare, constituting less than 10 percent of the total.[185]

Who, then, is likely to be deterred by the distant threat of the execution chamber? Probably not the person who acts in the heat of passion or the person whose attempt at robbery goes tragically wrong. Certainly not the insane or mentally disturbed killer or the person whose mind is clouded by alcohol or drugs at the time of the murder. Not the young gang member whose whole sub-culture exalts macho displays and risk-taking. Not the person who kills spontaneously or accidentally in the midst of an altercation; not the murderer who wishes to be caught; not the criminal who believes he can escape arrest or conviction; not even the cold, calculating murderer who notices that the probability of execution is very low. In his book on death row, David Von Drehle reminds us that

> the reality, with few exceptions, is that murderers are not clear-thinking people. They are impulsive, self-centered, of-ten warped; overwhelmingly they are products of violent homes; frequently they are addled by booze or drugs; and most of them are deeply anti-social. The values and sanc-tions of society don't concern them. They kill out of mental illness, or sexual perversion, for instant gratification or sheer bloody-mindedness. Some murderers actually seem drawn to the death house.[186]

Deterrence theory owes its intuitive appeal to the fact that when most of us sit back in cool, rational reflection, we reason that the prospect of facing the executioner would prevent us from acting on the urge to kill. But very few people are engaged in rational reflection when they use a knife, a club, or a gun. Besides, most of us do not belong to the small minority of people who will commit a murder. Most of us would not murder even if mur-der carried a small punishment. We are not the ones who need to be restrained. Not only do we have a well-developed moral sense, we have learned to control our baser impulses. We also consider our lives to be worth living, and we have people we care about. We have a lot to lose.

The theory of deterrence rests on other dubious assumptions. It assumes that capital punishment is *uniquely* deterring, that execution is perceived to be a significantly harsher punishment than life imprisonment without parole. For those few murderers who carefully weigh one possibility against the other, we cannot predict which punishment will be judged to be more frightening. The prospect of living in a cage for decades, surrounded by other dangerous criminals and stripped of all important choices about how to spend your time, is probably at least as terrifying as the thought of being executed sometime in the distant future. As Cesare Beccaria argued, the "prolonged wretchedness" of a life in prison has a greater impact on the human mind than "the idea of death, which men always see in the hazy distance."[187]

Some who believe in the deterrent power of executions despite all evidence to the contrary would argue that we simply need to do the job better. That is, the death penalty could be transformed into an effective deterrent if we increased its severity, certainty, and swiftness. Of course, not much can be done to increase severity. We could turn back the clock and revive the torturous practices of breaking at the wheel, burning at the stake, and boiling in oil. But few Americans would countenance such cruelty, and, in fact, there is no evidence that such practices were any more effective as deterrents. So we are left with the two options of increasing certainty and increasing celerity.

The penalty of death has never been certain. The U.S. execution rate peaked in 1938, when just over 2 percent of homicides resulted in executions.[188] We haven't approached that level of certainty since. A return to that historically high level or even a level ten times higher is not likely to cause potential murderers to believe that the risk of execution is high.

We could, however, compress the length of time between conviction and execution. On average, condemned prisoners wait over eight years for their appointment with the executioner. There is no doubt that, in theory, executions could be swifter.

But theory always differs from practice. The price would be high, and the hypothesized increase in deterrence might not even materialize. Our system of capital punishment has evolved over many decades and should not be dismantled in the vain hope that some potential murders *might* be deterred. Questionable attempts to create a deterrent effect must be balanced against our tolerance for error and bias.

The changes in the legal system necessary to boost the deterrent power of capital punishment—simplifying capital trials, dramatically reducing the number of postconviction appeals, increasing the pain caused by executions, increasing the number of crimes eligible for the death penalty—would be draconian, morally unacceptable, and probably unconstitutional. These reforms would also increase the risk of wrongful conviction and execution while failing to reduce the most common capital crime: spontaneous murder committed in the heat of passion.

Another Possibility

Deterrence theorists have always naively assumed that the threat of the death penalty would suppress the murder rate. The evidence indicates they are wrong. Of course, logic suggests three other possibilities: (1) the death penalty has no effect on murder rates; (2) the death penalty increases the number of murders; and (3) the death penalty deters some types of murder and stimulates other types. It is the second possibility, known as brutalization, that we now turn to.

From the beginning, public officials saw signs that the death penalty does not deter. During public executions in early America and Europe, pickpockets feverishly worked the crowds, even though picking pockets was a crime punishable by death. "The thieves selected the moment when the strangled man was swinging above them as the happiest opportunity, because they knew that everybody's eyes were on that person and all were looking up."[189] The thieves somehow failed to absorb the intended message of the execution.

Not only did the bloody public executions of the past fail to deter, they churned up great violence in their wake. That was the principal reason why, despite great popularity, executions were removed from public view. Public executions were the scenes of drunkenness, revelry, fighting, and rioting. From the beginning, the spectacle of killing has brought out the worst in people and brought out the worst people. After standing among the spectators at a public execution in 1849, Charles Dickens described the scene:

> I believe that a sight so inconceivably awful as the wickedness and levity of the immense crowd collected at that execution this morning could be imagined by no man. . . . The horrors of the gibbet and of the crime which brought the wretched murderers to it faded in my mind before the atrocious bearing, looks, and language of the assembled spectators . . . thieves, low prostitutes, ruffians, and vagabonds of every kin, flocked on the ground with every variety of offensive and foul behavior.[190]

The wardens of modern American prisons have long recognized the incendiary potential of executions. Disciplinary problems and violent incidents rise during the days leading up to and following an execution. And the disruptive effects sometimes reach beyond the prison walls. Especially when an infamous killer is executed, rowdy crowds gather near the prison to cheer in approval when the death is announced. It is for these reasons that modern executions are held without fanfare, in the middle of the night when most people are asleep. Unseen executions create fewer disturbances. Public officials *say* they believe that executions deter, but they *act* as if they believe that executions brutalize.

Like hypotheses about deterrence, hypotheses about brutalization can be tested. A careful examination of the data collected to evaluate deterrence theory should reveal whether brutalization occurs. If there is validity to the claim that executions brutalize, murder rates ought to rise after executions. In a series of articles and books on precisely this question, the respected death-penalty scholar William Bowers has examined data from nearly seventy different studies of murder rates. His conclusion is that executions do increase murder rates and that "this effect is slight in magnitude (though not in consequence), that it occurs within the first month or two of an execution, and that it dissipates thereafter."[191] This small but consequential impact amounts to an average increase of one to four extra murders in the weeks after an execution. Bowers uncovered another intriguing trend: Although the number of murders tends to rise after any execution, the rise is greater when the execution is well publicized.

It appears that executions do communicate an important message. It just isn't the message lawmakers intend to communicate. Apparently the salient lesson is not "If you take a life you will lose your life" but instead, "It is acceptable to take the life of someone who has committed an egregious wrong against you." In fact, Bowers argues that the process of identification is likely to work in exactly the opposite direction from the one proposed by deterrence theory: "The potential murderer may equate someone who has greatly offended him—someone he hates, fears, or both—with the executed criminal. . . . Indeed, he himself may identify with the state as avenger; the execution may justify and reinforce his resolve to exact lethal vengeance."[192]

The psychology of brutalization is not yet entirely understood, but there are clues in the research on aggression and imitation. Perhaps people with a loose grip on sanity are the ones most influenced by an execution. Media accounts of the execution and stories about the condemned man may bring violent images and ideas to the minds of a few susceptible and potentially violent people. Some of these people may become morbidly obsessed with a murder. For those people who are already primed and ready to act violently, fascination with a murder or an execution may be enough to push barely repressed impulses to the surface. Some sociologists and psychiatrists have suggested that persons haunted by self-loathing may even see execution as a means of escape rather than as a dreaded punishment. For such people, the benefits of murder may become salient. "With the crime that leads to execution, the offender also strikes back at society or particular individuals. The execution will, of course, satisfy a guilt-inspired desire for punishment, and may also be seen as providing the opportunity to be seen and heard, an occasion to express resentment, alienation, and defiance."[193] Clearly, many murderers enjoy their time in the spotlight.

Although the psychological process by which executions stimulate murders needs more exploration, the finding of brutalization is far more consistent with the evidence than is deterrence theory. Certainly, we know that other forms of violence beget more violence: The assassination of John F. Kennedy boosted the homicide rate, and highly publicized suicides, like that of Marilyn Monroe, provoke a substantial increase in suicides. And, like the brutalization effect produced by executions, the effects of assassinations and suicides subside after a month or two. The impact of all forms of violence is magnified when the violence receives greater publicity.[194]

Even if there is a deterrent effect (perhaps for the tiny percentage of murders that are calm and calculated), it is overshadowed by the destructive effects of brutalization. If a few innocent lives are saved, many more innocent lives are sacrificed. And if executions lead to the taking of innocent lives, surely the practice of killing murderers should be judged immoral, especially for those whose support of the death penalty rests on the belief that it saves lives.

All but the most irrational supporters of capital punishment have lost faith in deterrence. Those who genuinely believe in deterrence theory will usually abandon their belief when they become aware of the impressive evidence refuting it. But there has always been another group whose professed faith in deterrence was disingenuous. For this group, deterrence is merely a socially acceptable, sanitized reason for supporting the death penalty. Deterrence theory allows them to cloak themselves in rationality and conceal the underlying reasons for their support. Research has now stripped away that cloak and exposed the real reasons for their support of the death penalty: rage and revenge.

On the eve of a recent execution in his state, the governor of California expressed a sentiment often repeated by supporters of the death penalty: "The death penalty is worth having even if it only saves a single innocent life." Is the converse also true? Should the death penalty be abolished if it incites the taking of a single innocent life?

Does the Public Support the Death Penalty?

While a public opinion poll obviously is of some assistance in indicating public acceptance or rejection of a specific penalty, its utility cannot be very great. . . . People who were fully informed as to the purposes of the death penalty and its liabilities would find the penalty shocking, unjust, and unacceptable.

—Justice Thurgood Marshall

Americans are devoted to the death penalty, or at least that's what we're told by the mass media. Nearly every article or news report on the topic proclaims that the penalty of death enjoys overwhelming public support. And, of course, these reports are true: When asked questions such as "Are you in favor of the death penalty for persons convicted of murder?" more than 70 percent of Americans declare their support. Apparently, those who believe that capital punishment should be abolished have the lost the battle for the hearts and minds of the American public.

The belief in broad, solid public support has consequences. Those who are entrusted to make decisions about the value of the death penalty often justify their decisions by proclaiming that they are carrying out the will of the people. Public opinion on the death penalty not only affects the actions of political candidates and office holders, it also affects the Supreme Court's judgments concerning what does and does not constitute cruel and unusual punishment. Thus, it is vital to understand the dynamics of public opinion on this issue.

In 1972, when the United States Supreme Court ruled that our system of deciding who should live and who should die was unconstitutionally arbitrary and discriminatory, the justices looked to community standards for guidance. As Justice Powell explained:

Members of this Court have recognized the dynamic nature of the prohibition against cruel and unusual punishments. The final meaning was not set in 1791. Rather, . . . the words of the Amendment are not precise, and their scope is not static. The Amendment must draw its meaning from the evolving standards of decency that mark the progress of a maturing society.[195]

Some justices relied on public-opinion surveys to assess prevailing standards of decency. Other justices looked to another source of information about community standards: the frequency with which juries handed out sentences of death. This data caused some justices to conclude that the death penalty violated the moral standards of the time:

The objective indicator of society's view of an unusually severe punishment is what society does with it, and today society will inflict death upon only a small sample of the eligible criminals. [Juries] . . . have been able to bring themselves to vote for death in a mere 100 or so cases among the thousands tried each year where the punishment is available. . . . At the very least, I must conclude that contemporary society views this punishment with substantial doubt.[196]

While the Supreme Court continues to pay some attention to public attitudes, its analyses of these attitudes tend to be cursory, quick to reconcile inconsistent data, and disinterested in underlying dynamics. Justices are facile in their ability to use the very same data to argue contradictory positions. At least for now, the Court has decided that capital punishment does not violate community standards.

But perhaps the justices, the politicians, the pundits, and the media have misread the public-opinion surveys. It may be, as one observer put it, that support for capital punishment is "a mile wide and an inch deep." Only a deeper analysis of the opinion data can reveal whether support for the death penalty is fragile or solid, shallow or deep, ephemeral or enduring.

What the Surveys Tell Us

The Gallup Organization began surveying public opinion on the death penalty in December 1936, after unprecedented levels of public attention were directed toward the execution of Bruno Hauptmann, the alleged murderer of the Lindbergh baby. At that time, 61 percent of those questioned indicated support for the death penalty and 39 percent indicated opposition (a "no opinion" category was not included). In recent times, the standard question asked is, Do you favor or oppose the death penalty for persons convicted of murder? The pattern of responses to this question has oscillated wildly over the past sixty years. The percentage of Americans favoring capital punishment declined through the 1950s and early 1960s. Support fell to its nadir in 1966, when only 42 percent favored the death penalty, and it peaked in 1988, when 79 percent of Americans expressed support. For the past decade the overall level of support has hovered near 70 percent.[197]

Some demographic characteristics are systematically related to attitudes toward capital punishment. Differences have been found for the categories of race, income, gender, and political orientation. On average, whites favor the death penalty by a margin of about 20 percent over blacks. Blacks are more likely than whites to indicate opposition to the death penalty by a margin of about 17 percent, and about 4 percent more blacks than whites express "no opinion." When respondents are partitioned into three income categories—top, middle, and bottom—those in the top income category are 14 percent more likely than people in the bottom category to support the death penalty. More males than females support the death penalty (by about 9 percentage points), and females are more likely to indicate opposition by a margin of 4 percent. Political orientation also makes a difference. At present, Americans of all political persuasions favor the death penalty, though Republicans favor it more strongly. Support is also stronger among people living in the South and the West, and among suburbanites. In sum, the people most likely to support the death penalty are middle-to-upper class, conservative, white, male, and suburban. Although this is not the group most likely to be victimized by violent criminals, it is the group most likely to be disturbed and angered by social upheaval and change.[198]

Despite the broad appeal of capital punishment, there is considerable softness to public support. There is a rather high percentage of undecideds, and public opinion has been highly unstable over time. Pollsters at the Gallup Organization have observed that "the trend of public opinion on capital punishment is among the most volatile in Gallup annals."[199] And there are other signs of weakness in support for the death penalty. The public has grave doubts about whether the death penalty is fairly applied—45 percent of Americans believe that a black person is more likely than a white person to receive the death penalty for the same crime, and 60 percent believe that poor people are more likely to be sentenced to death than wealthy people.[200] Unfortunately, too many surveys have used a superficial one-question approach, and there is considerable ambiguity in the nature of the question that has typically been asked. The meaning of general support or opposition is difficult to unravel because a host of crucial questions are left unanswered by most surveys. For example, Why do people support executions? Are supporters well informed about how the death penalty works? Are they aware of alternatives to capital punishment? Is there evidence of support for these alternatives?

The meaning of responses to a single survey question is uncertain. When people say that they support capital punishment, we do not know whether they mean that they favor executions for *every person* convicted of murder, we do not know if support extends to *all types* of murder (e.g., both aggravated and nonaggravated), and we do not know the *intensity* of support or opposition. Opinions expressed in response to a general survey question may indicate mild, unstable preferences or deeply held convictions. Although there have been efforts to probe more deeply into these attitudes, it is important to remember that most discussions of public opinion begin and end with a description of general levels of support or opposition.

Some surveys have asked people to indicate reasons for their support or opposition. Those who favor capital punishment give the following reasons: "a life for a life" (50 percent), deterrence (13 percent), elimination of the possibility of future violence by the offender (19 percent), and the cost of keeping the convicted person in prison for life (13 percent). Opponents of capital punishment cite the following reasons for their position: It is wrong to take a life (41 percent), punishment should be left to God (17 percent), people can be wrongly convicted (11 percent), executions do not deter (7 percent), and there is always the possibility of rehabilitation (6 percent).[201] The high cost of life imprisonment has gained the most as a reason cited for support of the death penalty, despite compelling evidence that the high cost of the death penalty should be a reason for opposition. And though deterrence is often cited as a basis for support, there is persuasive evidence that executions stimulate rather than deter murder.

The Dynamics of Public Opinion

There have been other shifts. For instance, among those who favor capital punishment, support for executing juveniles has surged. Thirty-five years ago, only 24 percent of the public believed that juveniles should receive the death penalty. By the late 1990s, 72 percent expressed a willingness to send adolescents to the execution chamber. For many Americans, the face of violent crime is the face of a teenager. Whereas official criminal statistics indicate that juveniles are responsible for only 13 percent of violent crimes, Americans estimate that juveniles are responsible for 43 percent.[202] The most dramatic shift has been the fading of deterrence as a justification and the ascendance of retribution. Twenty years ago most people claimed to support the death penalty because of a belief in deterrence. Since 1981, simple retribution has overtaken deterrence as the most common justification offered by supporters of the death penalty. The move away from deterrence and toward revenge as a reason for support could be due to an awareness of research indicating no deterrent effect. But that seems somewhat unlikely given the lack of public awareness of other research findings. It seems more likely that retribution was the real motive all along, and it has simply become more socially acceptable to admit to retribution as a reason for supporting executions.

For supporters of capital punishment, there is another benefit to the shift away from deterrence or any other pragmatic justification for capital punishment. If it is socially acceptable to support the death penalty for the sake of revenge—or some sanitized version of revenge like "a life for a life" or "retribution" or "killers deserve to die"—then no further argument is necessary. There is no need to consider evidence on deterrence or cost or discrimination. Evidence is irrelevant. Support is a matter of moral conviction. Unsettling facts about how the death penalty actually works in practice can be ignored, and one's critical capacities can be switched off.

Some researchers have found that support is substantially eroded when people are given information about the death penalty, while others have found that only people with weak to moderate preferences are persuaded by factual information that contradicts their beliefs.[203] People who are strong supporters of the death penalty are much less likely to be swayed by factual information. This general pattern holds for a variety of attitudes about important social issues; people whose opinions are extreme or rooted in strong emotions manage to remain unconvinced by even the most compelling evidence.

Soaring levels of public support are not grounded in factual knowledge about how the death penalty is administered. Most Americans are poorly informed about such issues as deterrence, the financial costs of capital punishment, discriminatory imposition of the death penalty, and the probability of wrongful conviction. If support is based on emotion instead of reason, then asking people to endorse one or more reasons for support or opposition may not be especially informative. Some researchers have even found that people responding to surveys simply endorse every reason that supports their position. That is, people who support the death penalty are likely to express a belief in deterrence, revenge, or any other justification offered them. Still, the belief in revenge is the factor that most clearly differentiates supporters from opponents. When given information challenging the effectiveness of the death penalty, those who believe most strongly in retribution show the least attitude change.

The percentage of people favoring capital punishment drops precipitously when concrete rather than abstract questions are asked. When presented with summaries of three aggravated murder cases, less than 15 percent of respondents said that they would vote for the death penalty. And only a small minority of people who favor the death penalty would be willing to take an active role in its administration by being part of a jury that sentences a defendant in a capital trial or by helping to carry out an execution.[204] Actual imposition of a death sentence in a specific case is not something that even strong supporters of capital punishment take lightly. Consistent with these findings is the fact that real capital juries—which must be comprised of people who are willing to consider the death penalty seriously—return death sentences in only about a third of capital murder trials.

The unwillingness of jurors to impose the sentence of death

has been interpreted as an indicator of a deep ambivalence about the penalty. As Justice William Brennan explained:

> When an unusually severe punishment is authorized for wide-scale application but not, because of society's refusal, inflicted save in a few instances, the inference is compelling that there is a deep-seated reluctance to inflict it. Indeed, the likelihood is great that the punishment is tolerated only because of its disuse.[205]

The striking disparity between abstract approval for the death penalty and jurors' reluctance to impose it in actual cases was dramatically illustrated in the case of Susan Smith. In the summer of 1995, a jury in South Carolina sentenced Smith to life imprisonment for the murder of her two young sons, Michael, age three, and Alex, age fourteen months. On an October night, Susan Smith served a pizza dinner to her sons and, like any good mother, strapped her boys into their protective car seats before going for a drive. She drove to John Long Lake, got out of her car, shut the door, and let the car roll into the dark water of the lake. A videotaped reenactment of the event suggested that the car took about six minutes to sink beneath the surface of the water. After claiming for nine days that an African-American carjacker had driven off with her children, Smith confessed to committing the horrible crime.

In many ways, Smith's crime was among the worst of those eligible for the death penalty: It was a double murder, both victims were helpless children, and, perhaps worst of all, the killer was the very person the children relied on for love and protection. The murder was apparently calculated, not an impulsive act in the heat of passion. If anyone deserved the death penalty, surely Smith did. Yet, despite the monstrous nature of the crime, the same jury that had convicted her in less than three hours just as swiftly decided to spare her life. As one juror put it, "We all felt like Susan was a really disturbed person. Giving her the death penalty wouldn't serve justice."[206] As with many capital cases, a majority of the public disagreed with the sentence. In this highly publicized case, the public heard much of the testimony and arguments made in the courtroom. Apparently, this information did weaken public support for executing Susan Smith. However, even after hearing about Smith's sordid life—which included the suicide of a father and repeated sexual molestation at the hands of her stepfather—a sizable majority of the public (63 percent) still said that Smith should be executed. Only 28 percent agreed with the sentence recommended by the jury.[207]

In one critical respect, jurors in the Smith case were like most jurors in capital cases. They heard unsettling details of the tragic, twisted life of the defendant. They heard about family tragedies, physical and sexual abuse, poverty and neglect. And like most jurors, they found a reason to show compassion. Although jurors express abstract support for the death penalty, most will choose to spare the particular defendant they are called upon to judge. It is much easier to support an execution in the abstract, much easier to demand executions from a safe distance.

What Drives Public Support?

In one sense, the passionate debate over capital punishment is curious: Executions have a direct effect on only a minuscule percentage of the American public. Very few Americans are murderers, victims of murderers, or friends and family of either group. Also, opinions about the death penalty are in the main not formed on the basis of a careful and systematic examination of relevant data. Most people know very little about our system of capital punishment. Any attempt to understand the basis of expressed support for capital punishment must take these peculiar facts into account.

One straightforward explanation is that public support for

capital punishment is propelled by the rate—or, more precisely, the perceived rate—of violent crime in America. This explanation fits the data nicely: The trend line for support of the death penalty shadows the trend line for violent crime. Support dropped during a period when violent crime was relatively low (i.e., the mid-fifties to late sixties), then rose from 1968 to the early eighties as the violent crime rate pressed upwards. The year 1968 is notable because in local and national elections, street crime and law and order became major campaign themes. Since the mid-eighties, support has stabilized along with the rate of violent crime.[208] By proclaiming support for capital punishment, citizens are able to give expression to their anger and frustration about the rising tide of violence. With apparently little headway being made against violent criminals, the public is willing to go farther to crack down on crime. At least in the abstract, the death penalty seems decisive and final.

Some researchers argue that support for the death penalty is best understood as a symbolic attitude. According to this view, one's attitude toward the death penalty is a matter of self-definition. The purpose is to express support for stronger methods of crime control and to express frustration with the apparent impotence of our criminal justice system. Symbolic attitudes are part of an underlying ideology and are "tightly bound up with deeply held convictions concerning the proper organization of society."[209]

Significantly, declarations of support for the death penalty rest on emotion rather than reason. They are a means of venting anger, a demand that decisive action be taken against violent criminals, a desperate attempt to reassert social order. Support for capital punishment may give voice to both the desire for protection and the desire for revenge.

Support for Alternative Punishments

Usually, voters or elected officials choose between two or more alternatives. Yet, until quite recently, most surveys failed to ask about alternative punishments. Conspicuously absent from most surveys are questions about reasonable alternative punishments such as life imprisonment without the possibility of parole (the alternative sentence in most states). Perhaps Americans are receptive to such alternatives. Maybe they would even prefer them. By asking people to choose between alternatives, it is possible to strip away some of the symbolism that accompanies the death penalty and uncover what people want in concrete, practical terms. Beginning in the late 1980s and continuing in the 1990s, a series of statewide and national surveys began to ask people to choose among punishments for murderers. This simple innovation exposed deep ambivalence about use of the death penalty.

It turns out that support for capital punishment plunges when alternatives are presented. Public opinion is about evenly split when respondents are simply asked to choose between life imprisonment without the possibility of parole (LWOP) and the death penalty. That is, more than 20 percent of those who would have expressed support for capital punishment switch to LWOP when given the chance. Here are the percentages of the public endorsing LWOP as compared to the percentages still supporting the death penalty in several states: Arkansas, 49 percent versus 45 percent; Georgia, 44 percent versus 46 percent; Indiana, 45 percent versus 40 percent; Kansas, 47 percent versus 49 percent; Kentucky, 46 percent versus 36 percent; Massachusetts, 54 percent versus 38 percent; and Oklahoma, 49 percent versus 48 percent.[210] These findings have two interesting implications: Support is much weaker than commonly supposed, and it appears that most Americans wrongly believe that persons convicted of capital murder are eligible for parole in most states. That is, people don't believe that life imprisonment means that convicted murderers will never be released from prison. In one recent study, only

4 percent of Americans believed that a life sentence meant that murderers actually spent the rest of their lives in prison. When respondents were asked to estimate the length of a life sentence, the overall average was 15.6 years.[211] In surveys conducted in New York, Nebraska, Kansas, and Massachusetts, the median estimate was 10 to 14 years. In most states with the death penalty, the *only* alternative punishment under current law is LWOP. But few Americans realize this. It appears that the public strongly favors the death penalty only when the alternative is a prison term that allows for parole.

Concern about the possibility of parole is a pivotal consideration for a very important segment of the public: the jurors who must actually decide whether a defendant should be sentenced to life imprisonment or death. In post-sentencing interviews, most jurors expressed the belief that, for the defendant they judged, the actual sentence would be more lenient than the one they voted for. Specifically, jurors who voted for life imprisonment believed that the defendant would eventually be paroled, and members of juries that voted for death believed that the execution would never occur. Here are some representative quotes from members of four juries[212]:

- "Because of our system, the way our system is now, life imprisonment doesn't mean life imprisonment. That was a very definite factor in deciding for the death penalty."
- "Most of the people that voted for the death sentence said, Who are you kidding. . . . Why don't you just vote for the death sentence? We know he's not going to get it. . . . We can sit here and vote for the death sentence—it doesn't mean that we're going to kill him."
- "I was convinced of it and I still am. . . . He's going to get out if you give him life imprisonment—he's going to get out. We all knew that. We talked about that. If I don't vote to kill this guy, then he's going to get out. The only way I can guarantee that he will stay in prison is to vote the death penalty."

- "If he got life imprisonment and got out in ten years or fifteen years for good behavior and goes out and does it again, how could we live with that?"

This basic finding—that jurors vastly underestimate the sentences that will be served by murderers spared the death penalty—has now been replicated with hundreds of jurors.[213] Juries that render a death verdict often do so because they believe it is the only way to guarantee that the murderer will remain in prison for the rest of his life.

Like the general public, jurors find LWOP appealing for a variety of reasons: It offers a good compromise between the death penalty and life in prison with parole, it achieves the goal of protecting society while avoiding the burden of responsibility for ordering the defendant's death, and it bypasses the costly and unpredictable process of appeals. Unfortunately, most judges refuse to reassure jurors that a defendant will never be released from prison if he is sentenced to LWOP. This practice may result in more death sentences, because juries often assume that a life sentence includes parole.

The comments of jurors echo the concerns of the American public. Americans doubt both the certainty of life imprisonment and the certainty of the death penalty. More generally, most citizens express a deep distrust of the criminal justice system and its capacity to deal effectively with violent criminals. The option of LWOP allows citizens and jurors to punish murderers severely and to protect society permanently. At the same time, LWOP frees jurors from the burden of having to decide whether someone should be sent to the execution chamber.

Roughly half of the American public prefers LWOP, while half prefers the death penalty. But there is another alternative to capital punishment, one that garners the support of a clear majority of Americans: life without the possibility of parole plus restitution (LWOP+R). LWOP+R includes a requirement that all or part

68144

of what the convicted murderer earns from prison labor goes into a victims' support fund or is paid to the murder victim's survivors. In every state where LWOP+R has been offered as an alternative to the death penalty, a majority of survey respondents said they'd prefer it: 62 percent in Arkansas, 51 percent in Georgia, 62 percent in Indiana, 66 percent in Kansas, 62 percent in New York, 49 percent in Florida, 67 percent in California, 64 percent in Nebraska, 59 percent in Virginia, 67 percent in Massachusetts, and 51 percent in Georgia.[214] Averaging across states, 75.1 percent of the American public say that they favor capital punishment for convicted murderers when the only choice is between support or opposition. But the average level of support plunges to 43.1 percent when people are asked whether they prefer LWOP or the death penalty, and support drops even farther, to 31.6 percent, when people are asked whether they prefer LWOP+R or the death penalty.

Recent surveys demonstrate that support for the death penalty is neither as deep nor as stable as most general surveys seem to indicate. The widely cited "overwhelming support" for the death penalty may be something of an epiphenomenon, visible only in response to a general survey question about abstract support or opposition.

The death penalty attracts public support because it is a symbol of severe punishment for murderers. But when we look beneath the surface, it appears that Americans are ready to consider or even embrace other harsh punishments for murderers. As the data on support for LWOP show, many people who declare support for the death penalty are simply saying that they want to make sure murderers are never allowed to walk the streets again. Many people see the death penalty as their only guarantee. Support for LWOP+R reveals that goals such as protection of society and restitution to victims may be as important as revenge and punishment. Indeed, the survey data indicate that the requirement of restitution is especially appealing. Of course, symbolism is also at work in the desire to make the murderer provide restitution for his or her crimes. Clearly, no amount of restitution can begin to compensate for the terrible agony caused by the death of a loved one, and in any case, prison wages are extremely low. What seems crucial to support for LWOP+R is that the focus is on permanently protecting society and making the criminal pay. The prisoner would never again be permitted to lead a normal life, and he (or in rare cases, she) would at least be giving something back to the society he damaged.

One of the oldest debates in criminal justice has to do with striking the ideal balance among several important goals: rehabilitation of the criminal, punishment, revenge, protecting society from criminals, and restitution to victims and society at large. But which of these goals should receive the highest priority? For less serious crimes, most people would endorse a policy that emphasizes restitution over punishment; a vandal could be made to paint over graffiti, or a petty thief might be made to pay for the stolen goods. But what about the most serious crime? Clearly, the response to murder must favor punishment and the protection of society.

The public is receptive to the alternative punishments of LWOP and LWOP+R because these alternatives offer important benefits. First, both avoid the unfair application of the death penalty that most people find troubling. More than three-quarters of Americans believe that the death penalty is arbitrary and unfair, and more than half say that they are "not personally comfortable with" or have "moral doubts" about the death penalty.[215] Because of these concerns and doubts, most Americans would prefer LWOP+R. Clearly, this does not mean that Americans are willing to retreat from harsh punishment. Indeed, a second reason for support of LWOP or LWOP+R is that both are severe forms of punishment: Murderers will endure the hardships of prison for the rest of their lives. Third, both alternatives offer an ironclad guarantee that vicious murderers will never again walk outside prison walls. Finally, in the case of LWOP+R, the added requirement that convicted murderers work in prison for the benefit of society enhances its appeal. Restitution forces prisoners to pay for part of the cost of their own incarceration; it offers a vehicle for acknowledging the murder victim, and, in the optimal case, it forces prisoners to act responsibly and allows for repentance. And, although most Americans don't know it, LWOP+R is far less costly than capital punishment.

In pushing for executions and the expansion of the death penalty, politicians often declare that they are carrying out the will of the people. But the will of the people may be different from what politicians usually suppose. While citizens are not filling the streets to scream for abolition of the death penalty, the public is clearly receptive to meaningful alternative punishments. What is necessary now is for our duly elected leaders to show the courage to propose alternative punishments and to engage the public in a discussion of the real costs and illusory benefits of capital punishment. There is no doubt that violence in America is a serious problem or that murderers deserve severe punishment. But the problem is made more serious by the use of the death penalty. By abandoning the failed policy of killing murderers, we could expand public discourse and focus on the prevention of crime instead of the craving for revenge.

CHAPTER EIGHT

Is Killing Murderers Morally Justified?

With every cell in my being, and with every fibre of my memory,
I oppose the death penalty in all forms.

—*Elie Wiesel*

I do not know whether capital punishment should or should not
be abolished: for neither the natural light, nor Scripture, nor ec-
clesiastical authority seems to tell me.

—*C. S. Lewis*

When faced with compelling evidence that the death penalty
is costly, arbitrary, discriminatory, prone to error, and
without deterrent value, retentionists often retreat into the murky
waters of moral philosophy. They argue that capital punishment
is not only morally legitimate, but also morally necessary. Although we can decide questions of fact—questions about cost,
deterrence, fairness, and public opinion—by analyzing the relevant data, the question of whether the death penalty is ethically
justified cannot be answered by any amount of data. It is a matter
of faith and argument. And that is precisely why many supporters
of the death penalty would prefer to debate philosophy instead
of effectiveness. If we are morally compelled to kill those who
kill, further discussion of troublesome facts is irrelevant and unnecessary. Questions about how the death penalty is administered,
about the cost or the consequences of the penalty may be interesting, but they do not have the power to refute a moral imper-
ative.

The philosophical arguments surrounding capital punishment
are based on religious authority, moral philosophy, criminal responsibility, and concern for victims.

The Bible Tells Me So

In their final appeals to jurors, prosecutors in capital murder trials are fond of quoting Scripture to lend authority to their arguments. And there are many verses to choose from. In particular, the Old Testament seems to suggest killing as a response to a variety of crimes. The most popular quotation is from Deuteronomy (19:21): "Life for life, eye for eye, tooth for tooth, hand for hand, foot for foot." Moreover, the Old Testament recommends death for an assortment of crimes, including murder, contempt for parental authority, defiling sacred places or objects, kidnapping for ransom, sorcery, bestiality, worshiping false gods, profaning the Sabbath, adultery, incest, homosexuality, blasphemy, bearing false witness in court, harlotry, negligence that results in a death, and false prophesy.[216]

Yet, despite the apparent biblical endorsement of executions, there is much even in the Old Testament to suggest that killing may not be the appropriate penalty for murder. God did not kill Cain for the murder of Abel, and several cities of refuge were established so that wrongdoers could escape vengeance at the hands of the victims' families. The idea that "vengeance belongs to the Lord" and that we should "love our neighbor as ourselves" are major themes of the Old Testament. Even the often misinterpreted "eye for an eye" passage was meant to *restrain* rather than to *require* vengeance. Religious scholars point out that, taken in context, the passage does not tell us that we must exact proportional revenge, but that we may not take from others more than has been taken from us, that we must resist the urge to retaliate with ever greater violence.[217] *Lex talionis*, the doctrine of legal retaliation, represented an advance, a movement away from unrestrained retaliation.

Though the Old Testament authorizes executions in principle, in practice "there were such extensive procedural requirements for the imposition of the death penalty that, by design, it was nearly impossible to secure a death verdict."[218] Mosaic law and, later, the Rabbinic tradition established a nearly unreachable standard of proof. In the Talmudic courts (called Sanhedrins) two witnesses judged to be competent had to testify that they saw the accused commit the crime after being forewarned that the act was illegal and punishable by death. Confessions were inadmissible. So was testimony against the defendant by family members of the victim or persons with a preexisting grievance against the defendant. If any aspect of the evidence or testimony was found to be unreliable, the defendant could not be killed. Such restrictions served to make capital punishment extremely rare under Talmudic law.[219]

For Christians, the Old Testament must be interpreted in light of the New Testament, which goes much farther in repudiating revenge: "You have heard that it was said, 'An eye for an eye and a tooth for a tooth.' But I say to you, do not resist one who is evil. But if any one strikes you on the right cheek, turn to him the other also" (Matthew 5:38–41). The New Testament emphasizes love, compassion, mercy, charity, forgiveness. And, if we are to follow the example of Christ, forgiveness and compassion are especially important when dealing with criminals and outcasts. When Christ was confronted with a woman convicted of adultery (a capital crime at the time), the crowd who had assembled to stone her asked, "Teacher, this woman hath been taken in adultery, in the very act. Now the law of Moses commanded us to stone such: What then sayest thou of her?" In response, Jesus "lifted up himself and said unto them, 'He that is without sin among you, let him cast the first stone' (John 8:3–11). The same message can be found in Luke: "Judge not and you will not be judged; condemn not, and you will not be condemned; forgive, and you will be forgiven" (6:37). The entire life and teachings of Jesus argue against killing as a form of punishment. Though not a theologian, Charles Dickens made the point well:

Though every other man who wields a pen should turn himself into a commentator on the scriptures—not all their united efforts could persuade me that executions are a Christian law. . . . If any text appeared to justify the claim, I would reject that limited appeal, and rest upon the character of the Redeemer and the great scheme of His religion.[220]

Although the Bible can be read to support the death penalty, this support is subject to severe restrictions. Specifically, guilt must be certain and execution must be necessary to serve the interests of justice (e.g., to protect others or to instill respect for moral authority).[221] Indeed, no less an authority than Pope John Paul II has observed that the necessary requirements for the death penalty are seldom, if ever, met. In "Evangelium Vitae" (The Gospel of Life) the pope argues that "as explicitly formulated, the precept 'You shall not kill' is strongly negative: it indicates the extreme limit which can never be exceeded."[222] John Paul II goes on to note that punishment

ought not go to the extreme of executing the offender except in cases of absolute necessity: in other words, when it would not be possible otherwise to defend society. Today, however, as a result of steady improvements in the organization of the penal system, such cases are very rare, if not practically nonexistent. . . . If bloodless means are sufficient to defend human lives against an aggressor and to protect public order and the safety of persons, public authority must limit itself to such means.[223]

The pope is not a lone voice among religious leaders. Religious organizations are nearly unanimous in their condemnation of capital punishment. More than forty such organizations (including American Baptists, Catholics, Episcopalians, Jews, Lutherans,

Mennonites, Methodists, Presbyterians, Quakers, and Unitarians) have issued statements calling for the abolition of capital punishment.

Moral Philosophy and the Functions of Punishment

When measured against the usual standards for evaluating punishment, the death penalty doesn't make much sense. Obviously, killing a prisoner eliminates the possibility of rehabilitation; a corpse cannot go on to lead a more virtuous life. The goal of incapacitation is not advanced: the condemned man is already safely behind prison walls, unable to commit further crimes in free society. The supposed deterrent effect is illusory: as we have seen, executions appear actually to *increase* the level of violence in society. And since incapacitation and protection of society are just as effectively—and more cheaply—achieved through life imprisonment, killing the prisoner is simply unnecessary.

Moreover, how does the notion of killing murderers square with the cherished principle of "the sanctity of human life"? This idea is central to the world's great religions as well as the ancient Greek, Egyptian, Persian, and Babylonian moral philosophers. If life is sacred, it means that every person has the right to live simply by virtue of the fact that he or she is a living, breathing human being. This right is unearned and inalienable, in part because we are created "in the image of God." This basic principle certainly implies that the death penalty is morally wrong. However, three centuries ago, John Locke offered a classic defense of the death penalty on moral grounds. He argued that although the right to life is inherent and absolute, it is possible to "forfeit" one's right to life by committing a crime that "deserves death." His arguments have provided ammunition for supporters of capital punishment ever since. Locke also argued for severe punishment on the grounds of deterrence. He believed that we should punish "to the degree and with as much severity, as will suffice to make it an ill bargain to the offender, give him cause to repent, and terrify others from doing the like."[224]

Another influential moral argument is usually traced to Immanuel Kant. He believed that murderers must be killed based on the principle of "equal" or "just" retribution:

> What kind and what degree of punishment does public legal justice adopt as its principle and standard? None other than the principle of equality . . . any undeserved evil that you inflict on someone else among the people is one that you do to yourself. . . . Only the law of retribution can determine exactly the kind and degree of punishment.[225]

This idea has an elegant and appealing simplicity. It is an elaboration of the idea of *lex talionis* and is similar to the argument that murderers must be "paid back" in kind for their crimes. The principle of equality introduced by Kant seems to provide a standard that is independent of religious or political authority. And whereas Locke linked his notion of retribution to deterrence, Kant apparently felt that such practical considerations were not important enough to discuss.

Another argument offered in defense of the idea that justice requires the killing of murderers might be called the "moral solidarity" argument. If societies are held together, in part, by a shared consensus of what constitutes immoral behavior, then those who violate the moral order must be punished to restore moral balance in society. Further, for murderers, any punishment less than death is too weak to convey the strong sense of outrage and condemnation felt by the community. Only by killing the murderer can we repair the moral integrity of the larger community. In his book *For Capital Punishment*, Walter Berns puts it like this:

[The death penalty] serves to remind us of the majesty of the moral order that is embodied in our law and of the terrible consequences of its breach. . . . The criminal law must be made awful, by which I mean awe-inspiring, or commanding "profound respect or reverential fear." It must remind us of the moral order by which alone we can live as human beings.[226]

These arguments raise several questions. If by killing, murderers forfeit their right to live, does that mean that we are, in turn, *obliged* to kill them? Or will other forms of severe punishment suffice? If someone *deserves* to die, does it mean that we have the right to kill him? Should we try to induce in prisoners the equivalent amount of suffering they induced in their victims? Do executions really strengthen the moral solidarity of the community, or do they demean and corrupt the collective morality? Should executions be bloody, excruciating, and public to fully inspire awe and "reverential fear"? Is it necessary to kill in order to show that killing is wrong? And given the varied backgrounds and capacities of defendants, the diverse types of murder, and the limits of human understanding, is it even possible to decide fairly which murderers deserve to die?

The simplest counterargument is that, if killing is morally wrong, it is wrong for both the individual and the state. To be sure, there are circumstances where killing may be necessary, for example, when a police officer shoots a robber who is about to kill a clerk, when a soldier kills an enemy soldier during a time of war, when a woman shoots a violently abusive husband who is coming toward her brandishing a knife. These situations involve imminent danger, split-second decisions, and self-defense or defense of innocent others. Unlike police officers, who occasionally kill to protect their own lives or the lives of innocent people, the executioner performs an unnecessary killing, a killing that has nothing to do with self-defense, imminent danger, or the protection of society. The murderer has already been captured and waits in a prison cell safely isolated from the community.

The law of equal retribution proposed by Kant and others cannot be a literal prescription for how to punish violent criminals. We would find it morally repugnant to torture torturers, rape rapists, or terrorize terrorists. We do not try to kill murderers using the same method they used to kill their victims. Instead, we imprison them. Our efforts to mitigate punishments arise out the recognition that we must not sink to the level of the criminal; raping a rapist would debase us, weaken our moral solidarity, and undermine the moral authority of the state. We cannot simply respond to cruelty with our own acts of cruelty. Acts of brutality committed by the state in the name of justice never ennoble us. There must be severe punishment for horrible crimes, but that does not oblige us to kill those who have killed.

Try as we might, we can never sever the ties between moral concerns and practical realities. *Morality can only be assessed in practice.* Even if we accept the morality of the death penalty in the abstract, we must always look at how it is administered in the real world. Is the death penalty still moral if innocent people are sometimes convicted or executed? Is it still moral if the race of the murderer or the victim play a substantial role in determining which defendants will be sentenced to die? Is it still moral if the ultimate penalty squanders money that could be more productively spent on preventing crime? Is it still moral if executions provoke, rather than deter, violent criminals? These questions must be answered before any final judgment can be made about the morality of the death penalty. Moral theory must give way to moral practice, and abstract benefits must be balanced against tangible costs. Defenders of capital punishment must defend this punishment *as it exists* in the real world.

Moral Responsibility and Free Will

Suppose a man has been convicted of a murder. In a jealous rage, he rapes his ex-wife and then stabs her to death. Clearly, he must be severely punished for his horrible crime. He has shown that he is violent and society must be protected from him. His actions—rape and murder—legally qualify him for the death penalty. But before deciding whether he should die in the execution chamber or live out the rest of his life in prison, we must understand not only the crime, but also the criminal.

Here are four possibilities. First, suppose that he is a young man from a wealthy family who has enjoyed most of life's advantages: loving parents, material comfort, good schools, travel, and interesting experiences. Next, suppose that he is a young man with a brutal past: He and his mother suffered routine beatings from an abusive father throughout his childhood and into his adolescence. He grew up in a poverty-ridden, gang-infested neighborhood and received very little in the way of parental guidance or supervision. Third, suppose that he had an unremarkable middle-class background. He achieved his life's dream of becoming a police officer and was honored several times for his bravery. More than once he saved the lives of innocent bystanders. Or, finally, suppose that the killer is indisputably psychotic and that he had spent much of his life in mental institutions.

The striking differences in the backgrounds of these men raise some disturbing questions. Are all four men equally deserving of death? Are all four equally responsible for their crimes? If not equally responsible, is one of them, say, 90 percent responsible, another 80 percent, 70 percent, or 60 percent responsible? Should background even matter? Does the good service of the police officer count for anything or should all four men be treated the same? Would you be more inclined to show mercy if murderer number one was brain damaged? If murderer number two was a heroin addict? Any assessment of moral blameworthiness must go beyond the act for which a person is on trial. All systems of justice recognize this. That is not to say that the person's crime must be excused, or that the person must not be severely punished. He must be held accountable and he must be punished harshly. It is merely to say that even identical crimes may have very different causes and may be the product of very different life circumstances. We judge, convict, and punish a person. And a person— even a person who has committed a hideous crime—is more than the worst thing he or she has ever done. We are obligated to look not only at the vicious act, but also to struggle to understand the circumstances that produced the act, the reasons and motives that lie beneath it.

Supporters of capital punishment would argue that this is precisely the kind of information jurors are instructed to take into account when making the life-or-death decision. But the fact that jurors are told to take such information into account obscures the issue of our limited ability to understand the reasons behind someone else's actions. Imagine that you are a juror in a capital case. You have already decided that the defendant is guilty, and now you must decide whether he should be killed or sent to prison for the rest of his life. To decide whether to show mercy, you must make a full and fair assessment of the multitude of factors that led to the murder. To make this assessment, it is first necessary to have the defendant's important life events and experiences laid out before you: his upbringing, family environment, education, formative experiences, the things that shaped his character and behavior. You would also need to know something of his innate, inherited talents, abilities, and predilections. You would also need to have some understanding of how he responded to the events in his life, the impact of his experiences. Of course, it is impossible to know all of this. It is difficult enough to understand the behavior of people we have known for years. Even if we could manage to shut off our feelings of rage and revulsion, it would still be exceedingly difficult to find and consider enough information to allow us to fathom the reasons for a brutal murder. And, as a practical matter, no defendant or public defender can afford to present all the necessary information, and no set of jury instructions can adequately guide jurors in making this morally profound decision. Few defense attorneys even attempt to present sufficient information to make such an assessment.

Despite scientific advances in behavioral genetics and psychology, we are still a very long way from completely mapping out the motives, intentions, habits, interpretations, and situational pressures that propel a particular act of violence. The process is still mysterious. Perhaps if we had complete information and a year or two to sift through the information, we could arrive at a definitive answer to the question, Why did this person commit this terrible crime? But a thorough evaluation of moral culpability is clearly impossible within the constraints of the American courtroom. Some defenders present little information to help the jurors, and even the most careful defenders and prosecutors cannot uncover and present all of the reasons for the violent act. It is simply beyond human understanding. To believe that we can make such judgments is misguided hubris.

At the heart of the matter is an ancient and unresolvable philosophical debate: Free will versus determinism. Without at least an assumption of free will there can be no discussion of ethical behavior or criminal responsibility. Nearly all of us believe in some measure of free will, but we are all partly determinists too. Do you or do you not believe that you are a product of your genetic endowment and your life experiences? If you believe that your behavior is a function of inheritance and experience, you are, at least, a limited determinist, what William James, the great philosopher and psychologist, might have called a "soft determinist." Whereas the "hard determinist" insists that our actions are entirely determined, that no one is free to act differently from the way he or she does act, the soft determinist believes that we possess free will within the constraints imposed by heredity and environment. That, although our actions are not fully determined, our actions are strongly influenced by our conditioning, our values and habits, and the situations we find ourselves in.

In discussing the reasons behind criminal behavior, Stephen Nathanson argues that we must take into account the effort required by a criminal to resist criminal actions and the obstacles to moral behavior encountered by the criminal:

> A person's degree of moral desert is determined by considerations of what could reasonably be expected of him. If a person faces such powerful obstacles to moral behavior that it would require extraordinary amounts of effort to act well, then, though he acts badly, he is not morally to blame . . . different behavior could not reasonably be expected. The causes of difficulty need not be environmental. They could be physical, psychological, or of any sort, but if they make alternative actions extremely difficult or impossible, a person is not fully blameworthy for his deeds, even if they were wrong acts triggered by bad motives.[227]

The philosopher Jeffrey Reiman takes an even broader view suggesting that the larger society must bear some responsibility for the actions of murderers.[228] America spawns more vicious murderers than any other "civilized" country on earth. The social conditions that predictably produce violent offenders (e.g., poverty, routine exposure to violence as a child, access to lethal weapons) are at least partly to blame. It has been said that each nation gets the criminals it deserves. Put differently, a society bears responsibility for violent criminals to the extent that it tolerates social conditions that predictably lead to violence. Until these conditions are remediated, some of the blame rests with the larger community.

Let me be clear: The argument is not that murderers should be excused for their crimes. They must be held accountable and punished severely. The argument is that we cannot possibly fathom the multiple and subtle influences that cause a particular behavior. Instead of pretending omniscience, we should be more humble about our capacity to understand fully why someone commits a horrible crime. We can and should send a dangerous criminal to prison for the rest of his or her life, but we should not presume to judge which people deserve to live and which deserve to die. Our judgments are bound to be faulty.

Just Revenge

Beneath the usual justifications for punishing criminals lurks a more visceral and potent motive for the death penalty: revenge. The desire to lash back at those who have harmed us has deep roots in our evolutionary past. It is a powerful human motive that must be taken seriously, but it is not a sufficient justification for killing. Although individually we all feel the primitive urge to exact revenge against those who harm us, collectively we must strive to be more rational, fair, moral, and humane than the criminals who commit the acts of violence or cruelty that we condemn. We all sympathize with a bereaved father who attempts to kill the man who murdered his child. But a group's craving for revenge is far less innocent and immediate, and far less justifiable. A victim's relative who attempts to kill a murderer commits a crime of passion motivated by rage and grief. In contrast, the process leading up to a state-sponsored killing is slow, deliberate, methodical, and largely stripped of human emotion. The anger of families of victims is understandable, but anger should not be the basis of social policy. A community's angry cry for killing a murderer is far uglier than the anger felt by an individual who has been wronged by another.

We have all felt wronged and we have all experienced the powerful emotions that drive the hunger for revenge. The urge to see a murderer killed is rooted in the rage and revulsion that most

Americans feel when they hear about a horrible, inexplicable murder. We empathize with the victim and the family of the victim, and we want to see the murderer pay dearly for his or her crime. In movies, operas, plays, and novels, exacting revenge on those who offend us is often portrayed as emotionally satisfying. But just because the appetite for revenge is real and powerful, that does not mean we should indulge our appetite or build it into our legal system. Justice must take precedence over revenge. Arthur Koestler made this point vividly: "Deep inside every civilized being there lurks a tiny Stone Age man, dangling a club to rob and rape, and screaming 'an eye for an eye.' But we would rather not have that little fur-clad figure dictate the law of the land."[229] Feelings of anger and revulsion at a horrible crime are understandably human and maybe even a healthy indication of concern for the welfare of others. However, even if we accept the legitimacy of anger, anger does not outweigh all other considerations. Feelings of outrage and the quest for revenge do not guarantee that punishments will be fairly or rationally imposed. Anger does not ensure justice; it is an obstacle to justice.

It would be immoral to execute everyone who kills another human being. Every legal system on earth recognizes this. Consequently, every nation with capital punishment must create some method of selecting out those killers who truly "deserve" to die. Because no selection process is perfect, bias, prejudice, and error creep into every system of capital punishment. If the morality of revenge and the morality of the death penalty are to be defended, the defense must be of the death penalty as it is administered in the real world. Too often, defenders of the death penalty argue for its morality in a theoretical, idealized world. The claim that killing is morally justified must be reconciled with disquieting facts: the inevitability of wrongful convictions, the reality of discrimination on the basis of wealth and race, the likelihood that executions increase the murder rate, the reality that millions of dollars must be squandered to bring about a single execution.

Killing is a morally acceptable penalty only if it is essential, and only if it provides substantial benefits that cannot be gained by any other means. Capital punishment is not just a moral abstraction. It is a reality that must be evaluated on the basis of benefits and costs.

What About the Victims?

Those who support the death penalty have a ready response to all the arguments against it: "What about the victims?" The question is full of implied meanings: that support for executions is based on selfless sympathy for the victims, that all families of victims of murder are entitled to (and find comfort in) the killing of the person convicted of murdering their loved one, that the abolitionists would be screaming for an execution if their loved ones had been brutally murdered. More fundamentally, the question is an attempt to control and limit the terms of the debate, a demand that we choose sides. The question implies that you must be either on the side of the victim and the victim's family or you must be on the side of the murderer. You must declare your allegiance: Are you pro-victim or pro-murderer?

If by killing a murderer we could resurrect the innocent victim, no one would oppose the death penalty. Unfortunately, there is nothing any of us can do to return the victim to the arms of his or her loved ones. The answer to the question, What about the victim? is not only that an execution will not restore the life of the victim; it is also that a state-sanctioned killing will debase us all and create a new set of victims: the murderer's family.

The wrenching loss of the victim's family cannot be fully appreciated by anyone who has not experienced it firsthand. Their suffering is unimaginable to most of us. "There is nothing to compare with the impact and profound shock of a sudden unexpected death,"[230] according to psychologists. Whereas the loved ones of people who die from illness may have an opportunity to grieve in advance and say good-bye to the dying person, there are no such opportunities for the families of murder victims. When the death is caused not by a tragic accident but by the actions of a murderer, the shock and pain are amplified. The survivors must not only deal with their loss, they must also find ways of dealing with feelings of rage and hatred for the murderer.

It is widely presumed that families of murder victims are uniformly in favor of executions and that execution of the murderer facilitates the healing process. These assumptions may sometimes be true. After witnessing an execution, one relative of a murder victim described the event as therapeutic: "It was spiritual. When he [the condemned man] leaned over for the last time, everything I went there for just lifted off my shoulders. I felt peace . . . I have finality. . . . It was like a miracle of forgiveness."[231] We can only hope that her feelings of peace and forgiveness are lasting.

But the feelings and reactions of those who loved the victim are neither uniform nor predictable. For example, Coretta Scott King, who lost her husband (Dr. Martin Luther King, Jr.) and her mother-in-law to murder, said that "I stand firmly and unequivocally opposed to the death penalty for those convicted of capital offenses. An evil deed is not redeemed by an evil deed of retaliation. Justice is never advanced by the unnecessary taking of a human life. Morality is never upheld by legalized murder."[232] Some survivors of murder victims have even actively fought to thwart the state's efforts to kill the person who murdered their loved one.

There is at least one national organization—Murder Victims' Families for Reconciliation (MVFR)—comprised of people who have lost family members to violent crime but nonetheless advocate abolition of the death penalty. Their fundamental belief is that "healing happens not by vengeance but by reconciliation—with society, the community, the act of murder itself, and sometimes even with the offender." MVFR's founder, Marie Deans, posed the question, "How can we stand as murder victims, in our

pain and sorrow, and give it to someone else's family as well?"
She has also written that

> the hundreds of murder victims' families across the country
> who, to no avail, have pleaded for mercy for those who mur-
> dered their loved ones clearly demonstrate that the death
> penalty has nothing to do with the victims' families. . . . Vic-
> tims' families simply serve as a cover-up for the fact that
> our leaders choose to gain votes by reacting to people's fears
> rather than by honestly responding to society's needs.[233]

Oddile Stern, executive director of Parents of Murdered Children, opposes capital punishment and is "at peace" with the life
sentence received by her daughter's murderer. She feels that the
execution of a murderer "can never equate to the loss of your
child's life and the horrors of murder."[234] Sam Reese Sheppard,
whose pregnant mother was murdered when he was only seven
years old, calls the death penalty "a hate crime" and believes that
"it teaches that vengeance, hatred, and revenge are acceptable
values to be cultivated and lived by our society."[235] Indeed, many
relatives of murder victims show remarkable compassion and forgiveness:

> There is an old saying: "You would feel different if it hap-
> pened to you." Well, it did happen to me. . . . But after
> much thought and many tears I knew that my feelings on
> capital punishment had not changed. For I knew in my heart
> that killing is still wrong. . . . He must pay for what he did.
> But I don't wish him to be punished by death.[236]

For the families of most victims, the long, repetitive process
of trials and appeals may even divert them from the task of trying
to rebuild their devastated lives. The legal processes leading
up to an execution consume many years. Relatives who are

determined to bring about an execution must devote a considerable amount of time and attention to the task. They must listen to countless descriptions of the murder; describe their grief in front of attorneys, judges, and television cameras; and wait for years while the overburdened legal system makes a final determination. And even if the execution finally comes, they still must go on without their loved one. The long, slow process of trials and appeals, which often requires years of involvement by the victim's family, unnecessarily prolongs the terrible suffering created by a murder. Healing and recovery, according to the National Organization of Victim Assistance, come from "an increased remembrance of the victim—not the murder."[237] The police investigations, trials, appeals, clemency hearings, and meetings with legal personnel dredge up terrible memories time and again. Such events may prolong the mourning process and offer little relief from the pain of loss.

There is another set of victims: the murderer's family. A sentence of death creates additional suffering for the family of the condemned prisoner. The convict is always someone's son, and he is often a brother, a husband, or a father. The relatives of the condemned prisoner—who are often innocent of any wrongdoing—are swept into the widening circle of suffering created by a killing and a counterkilling. Mothers, fathers, sisters, brothers, spouses, and children wait for their loved one to be strapped down and killed by the state. In his moving book, *Shot in the Heart*, Mikal Gilmore describes the pain caused by the execution of his brother Gary:

> One moment you're forcing yourself to live through the hell of knowing that somebody you love is going to die in a known way, at a specific time and place, and that not only is there nothing you can do to change that, but that for the rest of your life, you will have to move around in a world that wanted this death to happen. You will have to walk past

people every day who were heartened by the killing of some-body in your family—somebody who had long ago been himself murdered emotionally. You will have to live in this world and either hate it or make peace with it, because it is the only world you will have available to live in.[238]

The shame and stigma of being related to someone on death row is painfully felt by the families of the condemned: "I've found that people can be very cruel when they learn you have an immediate family member on death row. Generally they leave you with the impression they think you are tainted because you are related to a convicted killer."[239] Albert Camus made the point eloquently: "The relatives of the condemned man then discover an excess of suffering that punishes them beyond all justice. A mother's or father's long months of waiting, the visiting-room, the artificial conversations filling up the brief moments spent with the condemned man, the visions of the execution are all tortures."[240]

Families of the condemned and families of the victim share an experience that is similar in some respects:

> The homicide victim dies by sudden, passionate, individual violence, while the condemned prisoner dies by slow, deliberate, and collective violence. The survivors of both must live with the knowledge that their relative died from the intentional acts of others.[241]

Studies of the families of death-row inmates reveal an agonizing mix of emotions: They feel angry that so many people want to see their loved one killed and they become acutely sensitive to how others view the impending execution; they swing between hope and despair as the appeals process progresses; they engage in self-recrimination about what they might have done to prevent the murder; they may be haunted by obsessive thoughts about the

murder and the execution to come; they grieve in anticipation of
the execution; they worry about the enduring impact the eventual
execution will have on them and other family members, especially
children. The condemned man's family must live with the loss of
someone they love. They must also live with the humiliation and
stigma of being related to a person deemed so vile that he had to
be exterminated. An execution may or may not bring solace to
the victim's family, but it surely enlarges the scope of suffering
to include the murderer's family.

It is critical to remember that even in years when executions
are relatively frequent, less than 1 percent of murderers end up
in the execution chamber. The other 99 percent of families of
victims must content themselves with a sentence less than death.
This creates yet another problem: Many families will feel cheated
because the person who murdered their loved one will never be
sent to the execution chamber. Other families will feel cheated if
a murderer *is* killed. Jeffrey Dahmer was sentenced to life imprisonment for a hideous string of killings. But after serving only
a couple years of his sentence, he was murdered by another inmate. The mother of one of Dahmer's victims was disappointed
by his killing. "It's not fair," she said. "His suffering is over now,
but we will suffer for the rest of our lives."[242] Instead of executing
a tiny percentage of murderers, we could choose to spend some
of the money now spent on capital punishment to provide emotional and financial assistance to the survivors of murder victims.

There is another sense in which executions don't serve the
interests of the victim's family. Executions often bestow celebrity
status on the condemned prisoner and draw attention away from
the victims. The victim's survivors often feel betrayed by the
courts and the media. You no doubt know the names of some of
the worst serial killers, and you may even know the name of some
condemned murderer who was recently executed in your state.
But do you know the names of any of their victims? As the execution date approaches, a condemned man often becomes the ob-

ject of sympathy. After all, he is about to be deliberately killed by the state in a carefully premeditated ritual at a specific, predetermined time. The worst murderers seem to enjoy the most notoriety, and their fame increases as their execution day approaches. Many receive bags of love letters and are sought after for interviews. While waiting on death row, John Wayne Gacy, our most prolific serial killer, produced oil paintings that were exhibited in New York and Los Angeles. He had his own 900 number where callers could listen to a twelve-minute statement by Gacy. There have been countless television shows and movies about serial killers, and each time another condemned prisoner is escorted to the execution chamber, his trip is accompanied by a flurry of publicity. One journalist, repulsed by the copious coverage of an execution, observed that the condemned man

> travels to his death on a crescendo of loud, ceremonious trumpets, full-blown biographies of his life and times and meticulous accounts of his final seconds. Yet his victims get barely a mention. Their murderer gets the cameras, headlines and team coverage, they get the fine print.[243]

Reporters and commentators are irresistibly drawn to executions and a significant segment of the American public is morbidly fascinated by the details of the murders, by the life of the murderer, and by the ritual of the execution. It is a tantalizing media opportunity: the drama of last-minute legal maneuvering, the countdown to the killing, the killer's final hours and last words, the reaction of the victim's family, the crowds of protestors and supporters singing and carrying signs outside the prison, the possibility of a bungled execution. Since the days of public hangings, it has never been otherwise. There will always be a depraved curiosity about murderers and executions. The only way to wipe away this ugly sensationalism is to dismantle the execution chambers.

CHAPTER NINE

The Politics and Future of Killing: Symbolism and Realism

I was in favor of the death penalty, and disposed to regard abolitionists as people whose hearts were bigger than their heads. Four
years of close study of the subject gradually dispelled that feeling.
In the end I became convinced that the abolitionists were right in
their conclusions . . . and that far from the sentimental approach
leading into their camp and the rational one into that of the supporters, it was the other way about.

—*Sir Ernest Gowers*

E ach year we send about 300 more inmates to death row.
Since 1990 we have executed, on average, about 34 people
per year. Even if we were to begin killing 100 inmates annually—
a very unlikely event—we would never eliminate the backlog.
The great majority of death-row inmates will not die at the hands
of the executioner. A few will have their convictions overturned,
many will have their sentences changed to life imprisonment,
many will die of natural causes. Our system of capital punishment
is little more than an elaborate, costly charade.

Ironically, if the floodgates were thrown open and hundreds of
prisoners were killed in a year, it would probably only hasten the
demise of capital punishment. We would see frequent accounts
in the media of state-sanctioned hangings, shootings, electrocu-
tions, gassings, and lethal injections. The men strapped down in
the execution chamber would be poor and disproportionately
dark-skinned, and their crimes would be indistinguishable from
those of many others who were given a life sentence or less. Some
would be innocent. Americans would be forced to confront the
death penalty as a practice rather than as an abstraction. Political

candidates would no longer be able simply to pledge their allegiance to the death penalty. They would have to defend capital punishment with all its costs, contradictions, and consequences.

In modern America, in the last few years of the twentieth century, abstract support for killing murderers remains strong, but the demand for carrying out executions is far weaker. Our ambivalence about executions seems to restrain us from executing more than a small fraction of the prisoners sentenced to death. For now, we can hide from the ugly realities of how death sentences are handed down and carried out. In states including Georgia, Florida, and Louisiana, a month or two of frequent executions has been followed by a precipitous drop in the number of executions. Our current system of frequent death sentences but infrequent executions allows us to preserve the symbolism of capital punishment without having to witness a bloodbath. Despite all the political bluster about being tough on crime, most politicians seem to understand that generalized support for the death penalty does not translate into enthusiasm for executions. In addition, courts are backlogged, prosecutors' offices are understaffed, and there is a severe shortage of attorneys who are willing or able to serve as defenders in capital trials. And, because a large number of death sentences are changed to LWOP on appeal, prosecutors often decide not to file capital charges unless a case is politically sensitive.[244] Clearing the road to the execution chamber will require political resolve and a massive infusion of resources, not just speeches or a few new federal laws.

Occasionally, we are able to see the performance of a grand morality play: a despicable murderer is killed by the state using modern "humane" methods. Good triumphs over evil. Unfortunately, the actors often spoil the drama by failing to follow the assigned script. The execution takes place nearly a decade after the conviction, investigations of the murderer's life reveal a shocking history of neglect and abuse, the murderer claims to be innocent, the evidence against him is ambiguous, the relatives of the murderer want to speak out on his behalf, the relatives of the victim don't want an execution, the murderer is insane or brain damaged or retarded. The show must still go on, but the moral is obscured.

Other Western Democracies

When we attempt to evaluate life in America, we compare ourselves to other industrialized democracies—Australia, Canada, England, New Zealand, and all of Western Europe. We look to these countries to see how we measure up on education, health care, economic productivity, and quality of life. We prefer to be in the company of other advanced, enlightened countries. But when it comes to the death penalty, the United States stands alone. Countries that share our cultural traditions have abolished it outright, or they reserve it for treason or wartime crimes. Most of the countries of Central and South America—Argentina, Bolivia, Brazil, Colombia, Costa Rica, Ecuador, El Salvador, Honduras, Mexico, Nicaragua, Panama, Paraguay, Peru, Uruguay, and Venezuela—have also abandoned it or permit it only for extraordinary crimes. Many countries refuse to extradite criminals to the United States if they might be eligible for the death penalty, and some countries donate money and legal aid to their citizens who face execution in the United States. By clinging to capital punishment we place ourselves in the company of some of the cruelest and most repressive governments in the world: China, Iraq, Iran, Libya, Nigeria, Uganda. Our continued use of killing as a form of punishment undermines our credibility when we try to champion human rights in other countries.

In 1995, South Africa closed another door to its repressive past by declaring the death penalty unconstitutional. Like many other countries, Germany and Italy among them, South Africa's experience with severe political repression helped to bring an end to capital punishment. Germany adopted a constitution that prohibited use of the death penalty after World War II. The Nazis had provided a disturbing demonstration of how the power to kill could be misused by governments. In the past thirty years only two countries, Argentina and Brazil, have reinstated the death penalty after abolishing it. These reinstatements "happened in the wake of military coups which had violated international law on many other grounds. The return of free democracies in both countries instantly brought about the repeal of capital punishment."[245] Brutal regimes always rely on the death penalty to solidify their power. One of the reasons why execution chambers still exist in America is that the United States has not experienced executions as an overt means of state oppression.

In other democracies, the death penalty is viewed as a basic human rights issue: Governments should not be granted the power to kill their own citizens except in rare cases of absolute necessity. As long as the death penalty exists, there is the possibility of abuse, a temptation to rely on killing as a solution to political problems. Opposition to the death penalty and support for human rights rest on the same underlying conception of the proper relationship between governments and individual citizens. That underlying conception emphasizes restraints on the power of governments to deprive individual citizens of life or liberty for political ends. In modern America, the only ends served by capital punishment are political ends.

Another difference between the United States and other democracies is that our legal system is more decentralized. Most of the criminal justice system is within the jurisdiction of individual states, so each state is able to choose whether to retain or abandon the death penalty. Although nearly four out of five states now allow the killing of prisoners, more than 75 percent of executions are carried out in five southern states: Texas, Virginia, Florida, Louisiana, and Georgia. These states fought vigorously to reinstate capital punishment in 1976, and, if the issue is left to the states, they will probably be among the last states to allow the practice of killing to die out. Yet despite state authority, the death penalty is still a national issue; questions about human rights, morality, cruelty, brutalization, cost, and fairness cross all state lines.

Toward Abolition

As societies evolve, the death penalty is applied to an increasingly narrow range of crimes. Eventually, it is used only for extraordinary crimes (e.g., treason) or for only the most egregious crimes, such as felony murder or multiple murder. Finally, it is abolished.[246] This suggests a useful detour that might be taken on the road to full abolition: restriction of the death penalty to multiple or serial murder. This restriction would mean that the execution chamber would be reserved for people like Ted Bundy, John Wayne Gacy, Jeffrey Dahmer, and Timothy McVeigh. There would be enormous advantages to such a system: Hundreds of millions of dollars would be saved; burdens on court time and personnel would be greatly eased; the risk of wrongful conviction would shrink dramatically because the evidence in multiple killings is often overwhelming; and racial bias could be greatly reduced because serial killers are almost exclusively white males. We could finally claim that only the worst of the worst are executed. Both supporters and opponents would have scored a partial victory. The major gain for death-penalty advocates would be that abolitionists would be deprived of some of their most compelling arguments. The new system would be much cheaper and fairer. For opponents of the death penalty, the most immediate gain would be that the number of death sentences would plummet by as much as 90 percent.[247]

For those of us who favor full abolition, this would be a less than perfect compromise because the state would still occasionally resort to killing. Objections based on morality and human rights would remain, though their force would be weakened. There

could be other problems. Executing only multiple murderers
would still be likely to boost the murder rate in the period following an execution. There is considerable evidence that, instead
of suppressing the murder rate, executions actually increase it.
Part of this effect can be attributed to the amount of publicity
produced by an execution. If we executed only multiple murderers, there would be a great surge of publicity surrounding every
execution. Executions would be novel events, there would be several families for reporters to interview, and the men sent to the
execution chamber would have been convicted of the most egregious murders. All this adds up to an irresistible story for journalists—ample material to work with, a life-and-death struggle,
and plenty of public interest.

It is impossible to predict how and when America will abandon
the death penalty, though some scenarios are more likely than
others. It is unlikely that the current Supreme Court will rule
that the death penalty is unconstitutional. In *McCleskey v. Kemp*
(1987), the Court dismissed compelling evidence of racial discrimination in the imposition of death sentences and suggested
that any attempt to abolish capital punishment should originate
in state legislatures. There is now abundant evidence of discrimination and arbitrariness in death sentencing and strong evidence that executions stimulate rather than deter murderers.
There is even evidence in public-opinion surveys that the death
penalty offends contemporary standards of fairness. All of this
evidence is more compelling than it was at the time of *Furman*.
The current Court has been willing to engage in elaborate con-
tortions to resist and then dismiss any evidence that the penalty
is administered in an unconstitutional manner.[248] The Court
has chosen to abdicate its moral authority and defer to state
legislatures. But the strong and consistent evidence cannot be
pushed aside forever. Eventually, through turnover on the Court
or by a change in the minds or the hearts of one or two of the

justices, the death penalty could be declared unconstitutional once again.

There are events that seem to presage abolition of the death penalty in most democracies. Some of these conditions have been described by Franklin Zimring and Gordon Hawkins: a period when executions become rare or cease entirely, although the punishment is still on the books; political leaders who actively seek abolition *despite* abstract public support for the death penalty; and national leaders who make explicit the link between executions and basic human rights, such as the right to life and the need to withhold from governments the right to kill for political purposes.[249] In other democracies, political and judicial leadership has been crucial. For example, in England, the death penalty was repealed in 1965, when 76 percent of the public favored retention.[250] This pattern holds true for most democracies (e.g., Canada and Germany); public support for the death penalty declines only *after* abolition. To be sure, politicians would rather have public opinion on their side. But usually public opinion is merely a convenient tool—useful when it agrees with the politician's views, ignored when it does not.

The president and state governors, as well as religious, human rights, and medical and legal organizations, could exert the moral leadership that might lead to abolition. Because it is both powerful and politically insulated, the Supreme Court may still be the best hope for full abolition. But even if the Court were to declare capital punishment unconstitutional—as it did in 1972—there might be another backlash against this federal intrusion unless political leaders and abolitionist organizations make the case against executions and help to temper the public's reaction.

The Politics of Killing

The death penalty survives because there are benefits associated with it. Two groups receive some benefit from the death penalty: the public and the politicians. For the public, the benefits are largely symbolic and illusory. Capital punishment enables citizens to vent their anger toward violent criminals, to express frustration with the impotence of the criminal justice system, and to satisfy the craving for revenge. Anger and fear are the emotions that energize public support for capital punishment. Social psychologists remind us that "anger is the most positive of the negative emotions, because it is the only one that confers a sense of power. When politicians argue, angrily, for the death penalty, they may communicate that they are in control, and at the same time arouse a satisfying sense of outrage and power in the voter."[251] Although an occasional execution may be emotionally satisfying for some and inspire a false sense of control, this benefit is purchased at a very high price.

For politicians who routinely invoke the symbolic power of capital punishment, the payoff is more tangible and immediate. By declaring support for capital punishment, ambitious politicians can quickly portray themselves as tough on crime. As Senator Daschle of South Dakota has observed, "We debate in codes, like the death penalty as a code for toughness on crime. . . . He who gets the code first wins."[252] The issue of capital punishment can be easily and effectively exploited for political gain. It has been a key issue in recent presidential elections and state gubernatorial races. Along with other symbolic issues, a candidate's position on the death penalty has been increasingly used to define candidates to voters. Politicians have enthusiastically embraced the death penalty and have frequently proposed that its use be expanded to a host of new crimes. And, in the United States, the death penalty is politicized at the lowest level—the trial level. Prosecutors and judges are elected in most states. For prosecutors who want to become judges, the publicity surrounding a capital murder trial can propel their political careers. They can be seen as anticrime warriors locked in a passionate struggle to send a vicious murderer to his death.

Although all but the most courageous politicians are skittish about proposing alternatives to the death penalty, survey research reveals a broad receptiveness to alternative punishments for murderers. Among the citizenry, there is a deep ambivalence about the death penalty. Juries are hesitant to impose it, and most Americans recognize that discrimination, inequity, and error are an inherent part of the system that sends some prisoners to their deaths. While there is no doubt that Americans want severe punishment for and protection from murderers, that does not mean that the public will settle only for killing them. Politicians have misread or purposely ignored the polls. Americans appear to favor the death penalty only if the alternative is life imprisonment *with* the possibility of parole.

The fight over capital punishment has launched and scuttled political careers. Americans place violent crime at or near the top of their lists of concerns, and the political rhetoric surrounding it is as superheated as it is superficial. Politicians are faced with a dilemma. In a ten-second sound bite they can declare their allegiance to the death penalty and show that they are angry with violent offenders. The argument for abolition takes more time and is more complex. A public declaration of opposition to the death penalty is seen as risky, perhaps even fatal, to a candidacy. Politicians are irresistibly drawn to any policy that appears to offer even a faint promise of turning back the tide of violent crime. In the abstract, the execution chamber is a shining symbol of America's resolve to deal decisively with violent criminals. Politicians gain a potent political weapon in exchange for pretending—in the face of massive evidence to the contrary—that the death penalty can be made to be effective and just.

This cynical manipulation of capital punishment trivializes the public's deep and justified concern about violent crime in America. Unfortunately, the political debate has bypassed a critical discussion of the costs and benefits associated with the death penalty.

In the war on crime, abolition has been portrayed as unilateral disarmament.

The policy of capital punishment costs more than just taxpayer dollars and court time. It has a huge social cost: It commandeers and corrupts our national debate over crime and punishment. It lets politicians off the hook. Meanwhile, politicians breathe a sigh of relief because they no longer have to address difficult problems or propose detailed solutions. Instead of a searching debate on how to prevent and respond to crime, candidates simply declare their eagerness for more executions. A productive discussion of the social conditions that spawn violent crime (e.g., poverty, hopelessness, unemployment, domestic violence, access to firearms) or effective responses to violence (e.g., enhanced crime detection, certainty of apprehension, rehabilitation, or restitution) is displaced by facile declarations of support for capital punishment. To politicians, the death penalty seems dramatic and forceful. More effective but politically unsexy measures are seldom even discussed. Executions thus become a sideshow designed to divert attention from the crisis in center ring: Although the death penalty appears to be a form of decisive action, it is merely a mask for inaction, an attempt to conceal failure.

The violent crime rate in the United States is several times higher than those of other Western nations. A probing debate about how to prevent and reduce violent crime is desperately needed. Instead, by focusing on the executions of a few individual murderers, we divert precious attention and resources from treating the causes of crime. Constructive reforms that carry the potential to reduce violent crime remain untried or are quickly abandoned. While funding for education, family support services, early intervention, and treatment programs dries up, tens of millions of dollars are squandered to preserve the penalty of death.

The death penalty is public property. We own it. Executions are carried out in our names, at our expense. Our political leaders owe us full disclosure of its costs and consequences. It is irresponsible to be willfully ignorant of how it is administered, to diligently avoid the troubling realities. The job of political leaders is to challenge or defend social policies as they are expressed *in practice*. Realities must take precedence over abstractions. If a policy harms public safety, wastes taxpayer money, and systematically discriminates, elected representatives are ethically obliged to change or abandon the policy.

Unencumbered by the facts, people scream for executions from a safe distance. Voices of opposition are effectively silenced because candidates and journalists are afraid to challenge what is viewed as an extremely popular policy. This silence produces a one-sided, one-dimensional debate, which only serves to strengthen abstract support of the death penalty. The public is led to believe that only soft-headed bleeding hearts could oppose executions and that evidence on costs and benefits is ambiguous or inconclusive.

The Role of the Media

Despite the high murder rate in the United States, few Americans are murderers or victims of murder or friends and family of either group. Thankfully, for most of us murder is an abstraction, a terrifying but remote possibility. Because of this lack of personal experience with murder, most Americans rely on the mass media for information about its prevalence. In many studies Americans vastly overestimate murder rates.[253] This overestimation effect is especially strong for heavy TV viewers.

This is not surprising. The mass media pours out a steady stream of violence. We can all switch on our TVs and watch thugs, perverts, rapists, terrorists, and serial killers any night of the week. The simplified and stereotyped portrayals of crime in newscasts and fictional programs create deep misconceptions and great fear. As fear and anxiety grow, the public becomes increasingly receptive to any policy that has even a remote chance of pushing back the perceived tidal wave of violence. It is at this point that the media and politicians enter into an implicit and destructive partnership: The fear instilled by the media is soothed by politicians who propose the death penalty as a simple and decisive solution to violent crime. As Glenn Pierce and Michael Radelet have argued, "In terms of political strategy, media-promoted stereotypes of criminals and crime are invaluable vehicles for politicians advocating capital punishment. A one-dimensional policy such as the death penalty seems justified if the crime problem it addresses is also one-dimensional and simple. If, on the other hand, crime is a highly complex and diverse phenomenon, an extraordinarily limited policy such as the death penalty is of little relevance."[254] The media presents a distorted, sensationalized, and excessively violent picture of life in America. Fear of violence fuels support for the death penalty, and politicians are delighted to capitalize on this fear.

The death penalty is the triumph of symbolism over realism. To say that public support is largely symbolic is not to say that hearts and minds cannot be swayed by new, compelling information. Attitudes are resistant to change but they are not unchangeable. If information about the costs and consequences of the death penalty became widely publicized, there might be a sizable shift in even abstract support. So far, the accumulated evidence against capital punishment has been relegated to the back pages. For the most part, the mainstream media confines its coverage of the death penalty to executions and political campaigns. As the number of executions increases, expanded coverage is reserved for botched executions or those involving infamous murderers. It is simply not the kind of coverage that stimulates probing discussions.

An Alternative to Killing: LWOP+R

According to Amnesty International, "The alternative to the death penalty, like the alternative to torture, is abolition."[255] But what would happen to convicted murderers if there were no more executions? There is already a realistic alternative to killing them: Life imprisonment without parole plus restitution (LWOP+R). If we tore down the execution chambers, people convicted of what are now capital crimes would receive an automatic sentence of LWOP+R. They would be forced to live out their lives within prison walls and would never be eligible for parole. In prison, they would be required to work to defray the costs of their own confinement, and a portion of their earnings would go to a victims' relief fund. Americans seem ready to embrace this alternative. As we have seen, detailed surveys of attitudes toward the death penalty show that Americans favor LWOP+R because it reduces the cost of incarceration, provides some form of restitution to victims, and is more likely to teach murderers to accept responsibility for their crimes.[256]

A sentence of LWOP has several advantages over a sentence of death. First, it takes effect as soon as the sentence is handed down. When no execution is at stake, the number of appeals is vastly reduced. Second, the community can rest assured that the murderer's fate is sealed and the victim's loved ones can begin to rebuild their devastated lives. Third, the convict sinks into the anonymity of a gray penitentiary instead of becoming a tragic celebrity battling to foil the state's efforts to kill him. Finally, LWOP is a harsh punishment by any measure. Perhaps some people feel that a life spent in prison, with or without hard labor, is too lenient a punishment for killers. A little imagination and a visit to any overcrowded American penitentiary should be sufficient to dispel that misconception. Murderers sentenced to LWOP would suffer all the pains of prison life: a bleak, barren environment; loss of control over all but the most trivial decisions; loss of contact with family and friends; crushing boredom;

and a grinding fear of other inmates and prison guards. This sense of fear and vulnerability would only grow as the prisoner ages and the prison fills up with younger, stronger inmates. All this without any hope of release. LWOP is the death penalty in passive form: God, not the state, decides when the inmate will die in prison.

If prisoners serving a sentence of LWOP were required to work, part of what they earned from prison labor could be contributed to a victims' assistance fund. This fund could be used to provide services and to ease the financial hardships on victims' families. Obviously, neither executions nor restitution payments nor any other form of punishment can ever begin to "repay" the victims' survivors. Prisoners are typically paid very little for their labor, so for any one prisoner the amount of money contributed to a victims' fund would be small. Still, a lifetime of labor multiplied by thousands of condemned prisoners could yield significant savings in the cost of incarceration, and could create a significant pool of money for victims' families. By adding an element of restitution to the sentence of convicted murderers, we could show that we despise murder but we respect human life.

It is not unrealistic to believe that the prisoners now condemned to die can be trusted to work. In Texas, doomed inmates are already working for the state. Some work as janitors or orderlies, but most work in the death-row garment factory. For more than a decade, death-row prisoners classified as "work capable" have been making sheets, towels, uniforms, diapers, tote bags, pants, and shirts. They sit behind sewing machines or cut up fabric according to state specifications. These inmates wield knives, scissors, and other potentially lethal tailoring tools. The garments made by the inmates are sold to state agencies and the profits are used to reduce the costs of imprisonment. There have been no serious violent incidents in the factory, and even minor infractions occur less than once a month.[257] There is a long waiting list of men who want to join the workforce, not to make money—they are paid nothing for their labor—but for the opportunity to socialize, to spend more than three hours a day outside their cells, and for the chance to prove that they are capable of useful activity. "The work program gives me a reason to get up in the morning," said one death-row prisoner. "If I were in segregation, I would probably sleep all day just trying to forget. It gives me a sense of dignity, doing something to completion."[258] There are also benefits for prison personnel. Prison guards report that working makes the inmates less dangerous. According to the president of the Association of State Correctional Administrators, "We know that inmate idleness is one of the precursors of inmate violence and other prison problems."[259]

Dangerousness

Some people argue that murderers should be killed because they might harm or kill inmates or prison personnel. After all, murderers have already been convicted of vicious crimes, and, since they will never be released from prison, they have nothing to lose. While it is true that a corpse can't commit further crimes, there is no evidence to suggest that inmates serving life sentences for murder are any more dangerous than the general prison population.[260] Although well-publicized serial murders come easily to mind, very few murderers kill more than once. Indeed, there is much evidence to suggest that "lifers" are far better behaved than the general prison population.[261] One survey of wardens found that lifers "are not a management problem" and that, instead, "they are a stabilizing influence in the institution."[262] Inmates vary in their adaptation to prison. Some murderers continue to be dangerous in prison; others are tamed and broken by the experience. Many murderers are weak and cowardly men who pulled a trigger during the commission of a robbery. Once they are placed in a prison cell they no longer pose a threat. The converse is also true: Some who enter prison for nonviolent offenses become murderous while in prison.

Lifers, like any other inmates, can be disciplined for any violation of rules. They can be confined to their cell, placed in isolation, or their minimal privileges can be revoked. Lifers recognize that the prison will always be their only home. They strive to create a predictable, secure environment because there is no prospect of release and there are heavy penalties for misbehavior. Past behavior on the outside is simply not a reliable predictor of behavior in prison. In fact, the only people in a good position to judge the dangerousness of inmates are correctional workers. In a system without capital punishment, local prison administrators would be allowed to decide which inmates pose security risks. These administrators would be granted the latitude to decide which prisoners should be placed in the limited number of high-security cells.

Because jurors are reluctant to impose a death sentence and a substantial number of death sentences are vacated on appeal, an LWOP+R sentence would be swifter, surer, and more final. The uniquely long and complex process of capital appeals would not be necessary. There would also be far more equity: Everyone convicted of aggravated murder would receive the same punishment regardless of race or wealth. Mistakes would still occur (although the chance of uncovering mistakes would be greater), but we would never again kill the wrong person or torture someone with the threat of execution.

The Message We Send

Much of the appeal of the death penalty lies in symbolism. But what message is sent by occasionally killing a killer? Killing is an odd way to show that killing is wrong, an odd way to show that society is just and humane. We intend to send the message that murderers will be killed and thereby to deter people who are contemplating murder. We intend to get revenge. Yet, despite our intentions, we also send the message that killing is an acceptable way of solving the problem of violence, that a life should be extinguished if we have the power to take it and the offender has taken a life. We lend legal authority to the dangerous idea that if someone has committed a depraved crime, we should treat him or her as a nonhuman who can be killed without remorse.

We could choose to react differently. We could refuse to respond to killers with a killing of our own. An execution is an endorsement of revenge, a statement that fear and anger ought to be granted full expression even when they decrease public safety. Blinded by the urge for revenge, we support a corrupt system of punishment. To preserve the primitive satisfaction gained from killing the occasional murderer, we are willing to tolerate an arbitrary, costly, discriminatory system that sometimes kills an innocent person. Renunciation of the death penalty would send a clearer, more constructive message: that we will not debase ourselves by killing, that the government should not have the power to kill its citizens, and that we are willing to forsake eye-for-an-eye revenge in favor of a fairer, cheaper, more humane alternative.

In part, the death penalty is a response to fear and social turbulence. As a leading scholar has pointed out, "It has flourished in America with the institution of slavery, with racial strife during Reconstruction, and with economic adversity at the time of the Great Depression, especially in the regions where these conditions were most keenly felt."[263] In contemporary America, where fear of violence has soared, executions reassure us that we are at least doing something. The morality play of trial and execution enables the public to believe that our legal system is, at least occasionally, capable of taking decisive action. The public ritual of arrest, conviction, sentencing, and execution are meant to reassure the public and give expression to their anger.

Unfortunately, the reality is that instead of protecting society and serving the ideal of justice, the death penalty harms public safety and contributes to injustice.

We do not allow executions to be broadcast on network television, or even on pay-per-view. The spectacle of televised executions would offend our collective sensibilities as a civilized people and expose executions as shameful and anachronistic rituals. The solution we endorse in the abstract is less appealing when it becomes a flesh-and-blood matter. When we kill a prisoner, we do it at night with only a small group of witnesses looking on. Few are allowed to see the prisoner strapped in, few get to see the needles inserted in his arms, few get to watch him die, few get to view the corpse. We take pains to hide the identity of the executioner, and we conduct the killing in an isolated wing of the prison. We have even tried to make the act of killing as palatable and "painless" as possible. Executions are now passionless bureaucratic rituals stripped of anger or excitement. They are the most methodical, cold-blooded, premeditated form of killing. To soothe any pangs of conscience, we remind ourselves of what the murderer did, and as the rage and revulsion rise up in us, we once again feel that executions are justified.

The influential anthropologist Bronislaw Malinowski argued that cultures turn to magic when knowledge and reason fail.[264] Other anthropologists have pointed out that executions are not unlike ancient human sacrifices. Both are wrapped in ritual: the last supper, the reading of the death warrant, the last walk, the visit with clergy, weighing and measuring of the doomed man. But the most fundamental similarity is that both are irrational attempts to alter mysterious and frightening forces, attempts by state officials to demonstrate that they are still in control. The killing of prisoners persists not because it stems the tide of violent crime, but because, like human sacrifice, it creates the comforting illusion that the state is taking action. Executions are acts of desperation, admissions of failure. Like human sacrifices, executions do not appease the gods, ward off the forces of evil, or restore social order. After the corpse has been carried from the execution chamber, we are less safe and less humane.

The United States is still bucking the worldwide trend toward abolition, a trend that is especially strong in open, democratic societies where there are ample opportunities to debate the utility and morality of different criminal sanctions. There is a strong, though not steady, tendency for punishments to become less harsh as societies evolve and moral sensibilities mature. Social upheaval, rising crime rates, or political demagoguery can slow, but not halt, this progress. Eventually, torture, killing, and the infliction of unnecessary suffering will come to be seen as morally repugnant. Suffering that serves no constructive purpose will come to be viewed as morally wrong, as will punishment that is inequitably applied. As societies mature, punishments are evaluated on the criteria of certainty, utility, humaneness, and fairness of application, not on hollow symbolism.

In Conclusion

Capital punishment is a failed social policy. As we begin the new millennium, we should abandon this relic of the barbaric past. Killing was once a public spectacle designed to terrify the masses and to demonstrate the fearsome power of the state. Today, we would find such spectacles vile and repugnant. If we want to be seen as a truly civilized country, we should not permit premeditated legal killing. No legal system is capable of deciding who should live and who should die in an infallible, evenhanded way. We should not pretend that ours can.

It is easy to support capital punishment in the abstract. It involves little thought and much emotion. It is far more difficult to support the death penalty as reality—a penalty that squanders taxpayer money and court time, a penalty that is routinely discriminatory, a penalty that increases violent crime and poisons our public discourse. In spite of evidence and history, supporters of capital punishment claim that all these problems can be fixed. But it is the reality that must be defended, not some fantasy world of ideal justice.

Support for the death penalty requires a sort of unthinking sentimentality. It requires an irrational faith that the government can select out those who should die without prejudice or mistake. It requires a belief that legal killings will magically suppress illegal killings. Most of all, it requires that we turn away from the facts and stubbornly refuse to look back.

Notes

Chapter 1: A Long Bloody Past

1. For a description of the early history of executions see Johnson (1990).
2. Anderson (1983).
3. Andrews (1991).
4. Abbott (1991).
5. Scott (1950).
6. Andrews (1991), p. 204.
7. Scott (1950). For a thorough account of the criminal trials and executions of animals, see Evans (1905).
8. Horwitz (1973).
9. Schneider and Smykla (1991). The most complete statistics on early executions are contained in the Espy file (Espy and Smykla, 1987).
10. Hook and Kahn (1989).
11. Bedau (1982).
12. Bowers (1984).
13. Horwitz (1973).
14. Bedau (1982).
15. Bowers (1984).
16. Costanzo and Costanzo (1992).
17. Scott (1950), p. 5.
18. Deut. 17:7.
19. Cohen (1988), p. 150.
20. Cohen (1988), p. 154.
21. Cohen (1988), p. 157.

22. Cohen (1988), p. 158.
23. Laurence (1931), p. 4.
24. Paley (1790), pp. 11–12.
25. Scott (1950), p. 8.
26. Cooper (1974), p. 27.
27. Amsterdam (1982), p. 347.
28. Costanzo and White (1994).
29. Quoted in Zimring and Hawkins (1986), p. 110.
30. Gross (1993).
31. Camus (1960).

Chapter 2: From Trial to Execution Chamber

32. *McGautha v. California* (1971), p. 204.
33. Woodward and Armstrong (1979).
34. *Woodson v. North Carolina* (1976), p. 303.
35. *Gregg v. Georgia* (1976); *Jurek v. Texas* (1976); *Profitt v. Florida* (1976).
36. *Gregg v. Georgia* (1976), p. 195.
37. *Gregg v. Georgia* (1976), p. 192.
38. *Lockett v. Ohio* (1978), p. 604.
39. *Eddings v. Oklahoma* (1984), p. 114.
40. Weisberg (1984), p. 344.
41. *Wainwright v. Witt* (1985).
42. Luginbuhl and Burkhead (1994), p. 107.
43. Ellsworth (1991); Robinson (1993).
44. Millman (1984).
45–54. These quotes from the closing arguments of defense and prosecuting attorneys originally appeared in Costanzo and Peterson (1994), pp. 134–143.
55. *Caldwell v. Mississippi* (1985), p. 333.
56. M. Costanzo and S. Costanzo (1994), p. 269.
57. M. Costanzo and S. Costanzo (1994), p. 269.

58. S. Costanzo and M. Costanzo (1994), p. 158.
59. Bigel (1991).
60, 61. California penalty-phase instructions.
62. S. Costanzo and M. Costanzo (1994), p. 160.
63. Haney, Sontag, and Costanzo (1994), p. 168.
64. People v. Kimble (1988), p. 507.
65. Press (1996).
66. Von Drehle (1995), p. 3.

Chapter 3: Is the Death Penalty Inhumane?

67. Amnesty International (1989).
68. Sahagun (1996).
69. Horwitz (1973).
70. Amnesty International (1989), p. 57.
71. Amnesty International (1989), p. 60.
72. Hillman (1993).
73. Amnesty International (1987), p. 115.
74. Royal Commission on Capital Punishment (1953), p. 91.
75. Amnesty International (1989), p. 58.
76. Trombley (1992), p. 14.
77. Trombley (1992), p. 14.
78. Trombley (1992), p. 29.
79. *Newsweek* (July 28, 1995), p. 22.
80. Hillman (1993).
81. *Chaney v. Heckler* (1983), pp. 1,177.
82. Von Drehle (1995), p. 126.
83. Abu-Jamal (1995), p. 10.
84. Abu-Jamal (1995), pp. 25–26.
85. Johnson (1990), p. 44.
86. *Callins v. Texas*, (1994), pp. 1,127.
87. Camus (1960), p. 199.
88. Johnson (1981), p. 49.

89. Amnesty International (1989), p. 62.
90. Amnesty International (1989), p. 64.
91. Johnson (1990), p. 67.
92. Johnson (1990), p. 83.
93. Cheevers (1996), p. A15.
94. Trombley (1992), p. 19.
95. Johnson (1990), p. 84.
96. Johnson (1990), p. 95.
97. Johnson (1990), p. 96.
98. Johnson (1990), p. 87.
99. Cabana (1995), p. 169.
100. Cabana (1995), p. 166.
101. Freinkel, Koopman, and Spiegel (1994).
102. American College of Physicians (1994).

Chapter 4: Is the Death Penalty Cheaper than Life Imprisonment?

103. Costanzo and Costanzo (1994).
104. Cavanaugh and Kleiman (1990).
105. Paternoster (1991).
106. Magagnini (1988).
107. Moran and Ellis (1989).
108. Von Drehle (1988).
109. Associated Press (1993).
110. Magagnini (1988).
111. Hoppe (1992).
112. Grothaus (1986).
113. Dieter (1992).
114. Cook and Slawson (1993).
115. Dieter (1992).
116. Garey (1985).
117. Garey (1985); Kaplan (1983).
118. Kaplan (1983); Spagenberg and Walsh (1989).

119. Haas and Inciardi (1988); Bowers (1984).
120. Spagenberg and Walsh (1989); Garey (1985).
121. Nakell (1987), p. 245.
122. For example, see *Barefoot v. Estelle* (1983); *Saffle v. Parks* (1990); *Clemons v. Mississippi* (1990).
123. *Thompson v. Oklahoma* (1988), p. 856.
124. Radelet and Vandiver (1983).
125. Baldus et al. (1990).
126. Paternoster and Kazyaka (1990).
127. Mello (1988).
128. Hansen (1996).
129. Greenberg (1982); Mello (1988).

Chapter 5: Is the Death Penalty Fairly Applied?

130. Newton and Frammolino (1994).
131. Feldman, Paul (1995).
132. Weinstein, Henry, and Abrahamson, Alan (1994).
133. Scheer, Robert (1995).
134. Bright (1995), p. 125.
135. Amnesty International (1987), p. 44.
136. Hanson, Christopher (1995).
137. Smolowe, Jill (1991).
138. Amnesty International (1987), p. 46.
139. Amnesty International (1987), p. 45.
140. Black (1974), pp. 90–91.
141. Bowers (1984), p. 142.
142. Cutler (1907), p. 622.
143. Wolfgang, M., and Riedel, M. (1973).
144. Greenfeld (1995).
145. Smolowe (1991).
146. Radelet (1989).
147. Paternoster and Kazyaka (1988).

148. Bienen et al. (1988).
149. Baldus, Woodworth, and Pulaski (1990).
150. Gross and Mauro (1989). Also see Paternoster (1991).
151. Bowers and Pierce (1980).
152. Gross and Mauro (1989).
153. Baldus, Woodworth, and Pulaski (1990); Paternoster and Kazyaka (1988).
154. Paternoster (1991).
155. Baldus, Pulaski, and Woodworth (1983); Baldus, Pulaski, and Woodworth (1985).
156. *McCleskey v. Kemp*, p. 293.
157. The full text of the resolution can be found through the ABA Web page at http://www.abanet.org/media/home. html.
158. Kolarik (1996); Uleman (1996).
159. Hubler (1993).
160. Castaneda (1995). Also see Rohde (1993).
161. Rohde (1993).
162. Manning (1995).
163. Radelet, Bedau, and Putnam (1992).
164. Radelet and Bedau, (1988).
165. See Borchard (1932) and Frank (1957) for a list of possible reforms.
166. Dolan (1995).
167. Reske (1995).

Chapter 6: Does the Death Penalty Deter Potential Murderers?

168. Hamilton (1854), p. 504.
169. Sellin (1980).
170. Peterson and Bailey (1988).
171. Lempert (1983), p. 112.
172. Archer and Gartner (1984), p. 132.

173. Baldus and Cole (1975).
174. Ehrlich (1975).
175. *Gregg v. Georgia* (1976), p. 185.
176. Klein (1978).
177. Dann (1935).
178. King (1978).
179. Bailey (1990).
180. Van den Haag and Conrad (1983), p. 234.
181. Sellin (1980); Bailey (1982); Bailey and Peterson (1987).
182. Bailey and Peterson (1994).
183. Bowers (1974), p. 163.
184. Koestler (1957), p. 57.
185. Bowers and Pierce (1980).
186. Von Drehle (1995), p. 209.
187. Beccaria (1764), p. 49.
188. Bowers and Pierce (1980).
189. Koestler (1957), p. 53.
190. Quoted in Laurence (1931), p. 209.
191. Bowers (1988), p. 71.
192. Bowers (1988), p. 54.
193. Bowers (1988), p. 56.
194. Berkowitz and Macaulay (1971).

Chapter 7: Does the Public Support the Death Penalty?

195. *Furman v. Georgia*, p. 429 (Powell, dissenting).
196. *Furman v. Georgia*, p. 299 (Brennan, dissenting).
197. Ellsworth and Gross (1994).
198. Bohm (1991); also see Fox, Radelet, and Bonsteel (1991).
199. Gallup (1987), p. 57.
200. Gallup and Newport (1991).
201. Gallup and Newport (1991).

202. Moore (1994).
203. Bohm and Aveni (1985); Ellsworth and Ross (1983).
204. Ellsworth and Ross (1983); Bohm (1991).
205. *Furman v. Georgia* (1972), p. 299 (Brennan, concurring).
206. Morganthau (1995), p. 23.
207. Morganthau (1995).
208. Page and Shapiro (1992).
209. Ellsworth and Ross (1983), p. 168.
210. Bowers, Vandiver, and Dugan (1994).
211. Dieter, R. C. (1993).
212. All of these quotes from jurors are taken from Costanzo and Costanzo (1994).
213. Bowers (1993).
214. Bowers, Vandiver, and Dugan (1994); Paternoster (1991).
215. Bowers, Vandiver, and Dugan (1994).

Chapter 8: Is Killing Murderers Morally Justified?

216. Bailey (1987), pp. 19–22; Melton (1989).
217. Cohn (1970).
218. Tabak and Lane (1989), p. 142.
219. Erez (1981).
220. Quoted in Koestler (1957), p. 99.
221. Bailey (1987).
222. John Paul II (1995), p. 96.
223. John Paul II (1995), p. 100.
224. Locke (1690).
225. Kant (1797), p. 101.
226. Berns (1979), p. 194.
227. Nathanson (1987), p. 89.
228. Reiman (1988).
229. Koestler (1957), p. 101.

230. Weizman and Kamm (1985), p. 71.
231. Wallace (1992), p. A10.
232. Tabak and Lane (1989), p. 130.
233. Kane (1986), p. 34.
234. Payton (1987), p. C7.
235. Sheppard (1995).
236. Kane (1986), p. 34.
237. Weizman and Kamm (1985), p. 73.
238. Gilmore (1994), p. 349.
239. Kane (1986), p. 35.
240. Camus (1960), p. 205.
241. Vandiver (1989), p. 128.
242. Justice files.
243. Rosenberg (1993), A14.

Chapter 9: The Politics and Future of Killing: Symbolism and Realism

244. Gross (1993).
245. Mayer-Schonberger (1990), p. 682.
246. Gorecki (1983).
247. Bedau (1987), p. 242.
248. Acker (1993); Ellsworth (1991); Diamond and Casper (1994).
249. Zimring and Hawkins (1986).
250. Gross (1993).
251. Ellsworth and Gross (1994), p. 45.
252. Dewar (1991), p. A1.
253. Slovic, Fischoff, and Litchtenstein (1982).
254. Pierce and Radelet (1991), p. 7.
255. Amnesty International (1989), p. 24.
256. Bowers, Vandiver, and Dugan (1994).
257. Clines (1994).

258. Marquart, Ekland-Olson, and Sorensen, (1994), p. 140.

259. Curriden (1995), p. 75.

260. Marquart, Ekland-Olson, and Sorensen, (1994).

261. MacKenzie and Goodstein (1985); Wright (1990).

262. Johnson (1990), p. 160.

263. Bowers, Pierce, and McDevitt (1984), p. 385.

264. Malinowski (1954).

References

Abbott, G. (1991). *Lords of the Scaffold*. New York: St. Martin's Press.

Abu-Jamal, M. (1995). *Live From Death Row*. Reading, Mass.: Addison-Wesley.

Acker, J. R. (1993). "A Different Agenda: The Supreme Court, Empirical Research Evidence, and Capital Punishment Decisions, 1986–1989." *Law and Society Review*, vol. 27, pp. 65–88.

American College of Physicians (1994). *Breach of Trust*. Philadelphia: American College of Physicians.

Amnesty International (1987). *United States of America: The Death Penalty*. Amnesty International USA.

Amnesty International (1995). *The Machinery of Death*. New York: Amnesty International USA.

Amnesty International (1989). *When the State Kills*. New York: Amnesty International USA.

Amsterdam, A. G. (1982). "Capital Punishment." In H. Bedau, *The Death Penalty in America*, pp. 346–358.

Andersen, K. (January 24, 1983). "An Eye for an Eye." *Time*, pp. 28–39.

Andrews, W. (1991). *Old Time Punishments*. New York: Dorset Press.

Archer, D., and Gartner, R. (1984). *Violence and Crime in Cross-National Perspective*. New Haven, Conn. Yale University Press.

Associated Press. (October 14, 1993). "Senate Will Debate Death Penalty Bill." *Beloit Daily News*, p. 11.

Bailey, L. R. (1987). *Capital Punishment: What the Bible Says*. Nashville: Abingdon Press.

Bailey, W. (1982). "Capital Punishment and Lethal Assaults Against Police." *Criminology*, vol. 19, pp. 608–625.

Bailey, W. (1990). "Murder, Capital Punishment, and Television: Execution Publicity and Homicide Rates." *American Sociological Review*, vol. 55, pp. 628–633.

Bailey, W. C., and Peterson, R. D. (1987). "Police Killings and Capital Punishment: The Post-Furman Period." *Criminology*, vol. 25, pp. 1–25.

Bailey, W. C., and Peterson, R. D. (1994). "Murder, Capital Punishment and Deterrence: A Review of the Evidence and an Examination of Police Killings." *Journal of Social Issues*, vol. 50, pp. 53–74.

Baldus, D. C., and Cole, J. W. (1975). "Statistical Evidence on the Deterrent Effect of Capital Punishment: A Comparison of the Work of Thorsten Sellin and Isaac Ehrlich." *Yale Law Journal*, vol. 85, pp. 170–186.

Baldus, D. C., Pulaski, C. L., and Woodworth, G. (1983). "Comparative Review of Death Sentences: An Empirical Study of the Georgia Experience." *Journal of Criminal Law and Criminology*, vol. 74, pp. 661–753.

Baldus, D. C., Pulaski, C. L., and Woodworth, G. (1985). "Monitoring and Evaluating Contemporary Death Sentencing

Systems: Lessons from Georgia." *University of California Davis Law Review*, vol. 18, pp. 1,375–1,407.

Baldus, D. C., Woodworth, G., and Pulaski, C. L. (1990). *Equal Justice and the Death Penalty: A Legal and Empirical Analysis.* Boston: Northeastern University Press.

Barefoot v. Estelle (1983), 463 U.S. 880.

Beccaria, C. (1764) (Reissued 1963). *On Crimes and Punishments.* Indianapolis: Bobbs-Merrill.

Bedau, H. A. (1987). *Death Is Different: Studies in the Morality, Law and Politics of Capital Punishment.* Boston: Northeastern University Press.

Bedau, H. A. (1982). *The Death Penalty in America.* New York: Oxford University Press.

Berger, V., Walthour, N., Dorn, A., Lindsey, D., Thompson, P., and Von Helms, B. (1989). "Too Much Justice?: A Legislative Response to *McCleskey v. Kemp.*" *Harvard Civil Rights Civil Liberties Law Review*, 24, pp. 437–528.

Berkowitz, L., and Macaulay, J. (1971). "The Contagion of Criminal Violence." *Sociometry*, vol. 34, pp. 238–260.

Berns, W. (1979). *For Capital Punishment.* New York: Basic Books.

Bienen, L. B., Weiner, N. A., Denno, D. W., Allison, P. D., Mills, D. L. (1988). "The Reimposition of Capital Punishment in New Jersey: The Role of Prosecutorial Discretion." *Rutgers Law Review*, vol. 41, pp. 27–172.

Bigel, A. (1991). "William H. Rehnquist on Capital Punishment." *Ohio Northern University Law Review*, vol. 17, pp. 729–768.

Black, C. L. (1974). *Capital Punishment: The Inevitability of Caprice and Mistake*. New York: W. W. Norton and Company.

Bohm, R. M. (1991). "American Death Penalty Opinion, 1936–1986: A Critical Examination of the Gallup Polls." In R. M. Bohm (ed.), *The Death Penalty in America: Current Research*. Cincinnati: Anderson.

Bohm, R. M., and Aveni, A. F. (1985). "Knowledge About the Death Penalty: A Test of the Marshall Hypothesis." Paper presented at the annual meeting of the American Society of Criminology, San Diego, Cal.

Borchard, E. (1932). *Convicting the Innocent*. New Haven: Yale University Press.

Bowers, W. J. (1993). "Capital Punishment and Contemporary Values: People's Misgivings and the Court's Misperceptions." *Law and Society Review*, 27, pp. 157–176.

Bowers, W. J. (1974). *Executions in America*. Lexington, Mass.: Lexington Books.

Bowers, W. J. (1988). "The Effect of Executions is Brutalization, Not Deterrence." In K. C. Haas and J. A. Inciardi (eds.) *Challenging Capital Punishment* (pp. 49–89). Newbury Park, Cal.: Sage.

Bowers, W. J. and Pierce, G. (1980). "Arbitrariness and Discrimination under Post-Furman Capital Statutes." *Crime and Delinquency*, vol. 26, pp. 563–576.

Bowers, W. J. with Pierce, G. L., and McDevitt, J. F. (1984). *Legal Homicide*. Boston: Northeastern University Press.

Bowers, W. J., Vandiver, M., and Dugan, P. H. (1994). "A New Look at Public Opinion on Capital Punishment: What Citizens and Legislators Prefer." *American Journal of Criminal Law*, vol. 22, pp. 77–150.

Bright, S. B. (1995). "Race, Poverty and Disadvantage in the Infliction of the Death Penalty in the Death Belt." In *The Machinery of Death*. Amnesty International USA.

Cabana, D. (1995). "The Executioner's Perspective." In *The Machinery of Death*. (pp. 163–171). New York: Amnesty International USA.

Caldwell v. Mississippi (1985). 472 U.S. 320.

Callins v. Texas (1994). 114 S.Ct. 1127.

Camus, A. (1960). "Reflections on the Guillotine." In *Resistance, Rebellion, and Death*. New York: Vintage.

Castaneda, C. J. (October 24, 1995). "Death Penalty Centers Losing Support, Funds." *USA Today*.

Cavanaugh, D. P., and Kleiman, M. A. (1990). *A Cost-Benefit Analysis of Prison Cell Construction and Alternative Sanctions*. Cambridge, Mass.: Botec Analysis.

Chaney v. Heckler (1983). 718 F.2d.

Cheevers, J. (January 15, 1996). "State Readies for First Execution by Lethal Injection." *Los Angeles Times*.

Clemons v. Mississippi (1990). 110 S.Ct. 1441.

Clines, F. X. (January 12, 1994). "Self-Esteem and Friendship in a Factory on Death Row." *The New York Times National*, pp. A1, A8.

Cohen, D. A. (1988). "In Defense of the Gallows." *American Quarterly*, vol. 40, pp. 147–164.

Cohn, H. (1970). "The Penology of the Talmud." *Israel Law Review*, vol. 5, pp. 451–463.

Cook, P. J. and Slawson, D. B. (1993). *The Costs of Processing Murder Cases in North Carolina*. Report to the North Carolina State Justice Institute.

Cooper, D. D. (1974). *The Lesson of the Scaffold*. Athens, Ohio: Ohio University Press.

Costanzo, M., and Costanzo, S. (1992). "Jury Decision Making in the Capital Penalty Phase: Legal Assumptions, Empirical Findings, and a Research Agenda." *Law and Human Behavior*, vol. 16. pp. 185–202.

Costanzo, M., and Costanzo, S. (1994). "The Death Penalty: Public Opinions, Legal Decisions, and Juror Perspectives." In M. Costanzo and S. Oskamp (eds.), *Violence and the Law* (pp. 246–271). Thousand Oaks, Cal.: Sage Publications.

Costanzo, M., and Peterson, J. (1994). "Attorney Persuasion in the Capital Penalty Phase: A Content Analysis of Closing Arguments." *Journal of Social Issues*, vol. 50, pp. 125–148.

Costanzo, M., and White, L. T. (1994). "An Overview of the Death Penalty and Capital Trials: History, Current Status, Legal Procedures, and Cost." *Journal of Social Issues*, vol. 50, pp. 1–18.

Costanzo, S., and Costanzo, M. (1994). "Life or Death Decisions: An Analysis of Capital Jury Decision-Making under the Special Issues Sentencing Framework." *Law and Human Behavior*, 18, pp. 151–170.

Curriden, M. (July 1995). "Hard Time." *ABA Journal*. pp. 70–75.

Cutler, J. E. (1907). "Capital Punishment and Lynchings." *The Annals*, vol. 29.

Dann, R. H. (1935). *The Deterrent Effect of Capital Punishment.* Friends Social Service Series.

Dewar, H. (November 26, 1991). "On Capital Hill, Symbols Triumph." *The Washington Post.* p. A1.

Diamond, S. S. and Casper, J. D. (1994). "Empirical Evidence and the Death Penalty: Past and Future." *Journal of Social Issues,* vol. 50, pp. 177–197.

Dieter, R. C. (1992). *Millions Misspent: What Politicians Don't Say About the High Costs of the Death Penalty.* Washington, D.C.: The Death Penalty Information Center.

Dieter, R. C. (1993). *Sentencing for Life: Americans Embrace Alternatives to the Death Penalty.* Washington, D.C.: The Death Penalty Information Center.

Dolan, M. (1995). "State High Court is Strong Enforcer of the Death Penalty." *Los Angeles Times.* p. A24.

Eddings v. Oklahoma (1982). p. 71. L. Ed. 2d 1.

Ehrlich, I. (1975). "The Deterrent Effect of Capital Punishment: A Question of Life and Death." *American Economic Review,* vol. 65, pp. 397–417.

Ellsworth, P. C. (1991). "To Tell What We Know or Wait for Godot?" *Law and Human Behavior,* 15, pp. 77–90.

Ellsworth, P. C. (1991). "Unpleasant Facts: The Supreme Court's Response to Empirical Research on the Death Penalty." In K. C. Haas and J. A. Inciardi (eds.), *Challenging Capital Punishment* (pp. 177–221). Newbury Park, Cal.: Sage.

Ellsworth, P. C., and Gross, S. R. (1994). "Hardening of the Attitudes: Americans' Views on the Death Penalty." *Journal of Social Issues,* vol. 50, pp. 19–52.

Ellsworth, P. C., and Ross, L. (1983). "Public Opinion and Capital Punishment: A Close Examination of the Views of Abolitionists and Retentionists." *Crime and Delinquency*, 29, pp. 116–169.

Erez, M. (1981). "Thou Shalt Not Execute: Hebrew Law Perspective on Capital Punishment." *Criminology*, vol. 19.

Espy, M. W., and Smykla, J. O. (1987). *Executions in the United States, 1608–1987: The Espy File*. Ann Arbor, Mich.: Interuniversity Consortium for Political and Social Research.

Evans, E. P. (1906). *The Criminal Prosecution and Capital Punishment of Animals*. London: Heinemann.

Feldman, P. (April 6, 1995). "The Mundane Murder Trial down the Hall." *Los Angeles Times*, p. A20.

Fox, J. A., Radelet, M. L., and Bonsteel, J. L. (1991). "Death Penalty Opinion in the Post-Furman Years." *New York University Review of Law and Social Change*, vol. 28, pp. 499–528.

Frank, J., and Frank, B. (1957). *Not Guilty*. Garden City, N.Y.: Doubleday.

Freinkel, A., Koopman, C., and Spiegel, D. (1994). "Dissociative Symptoms in Media Eyewitnesses of an Execution." *American Journal of Psychiatry*, vol. 151, pp. 1,335–1,339.

Gallup, G. H. (1987). *The Gallup Poll: Public Opinion 1986*. Wilmington, Del.: Scholarly Resources.

Gallup, A., and Newport, F. (1991, June). "Death Penalty Support Remains Strong." *The Gallup Poll Monthly*, 309, pp. 40–45.

Gardner v. Florida (1977). 430 U.S. 349.

Garey, M. (1985). "The Cost of Taking a Life: Dollars and Sense of the Death Penalty." *University of California Davis Law Review*, 18, pp. 1,221–1,270.

Gilmore, M. (1994). *Shot in the Heart*. New York: Doubleday.

Gorecki, J. (1983). *Capital Punishment: Criminal Law and Social Evolution*. Columbia University Press.

Greenberg, J. (1982). "Capital Punishment as a System." *Yale Law Journal*, vol. 91, p. 908.

Greenfeld, L. A. (October 1995). *Capital Punishment, 1994*. Washington, D.C.: Bureau of Justice Statistics.

Gregg v. Georgia (1976). 428 U.S. 153.

Gross, S. R. (1993). "The Romance of Revenge: Capital Punishment in America." *Studies in Law, Politics, and Society*, vol. 13, pp. 71–104.

Gross, S. R., and Mauro, R. (1989). *Death and Discrimination: Racial Disparities in Capital Sentencing*. Boston: Northeastern University Press.

Grothaus, D. (December 7, 1988). "Death, Dollars and Scales of Justice." *The Houston Post*, p. 3B.

Haas, K. C., and Inciardi, J. A. (1988). "Lingering Doubts About a Popular Punishment." In K. C. Haas and J. A. Inciardi (eds.), *Challenging Capital Punishment* (pp. 11–28). Newbury Park, Cal.: Sage.

Hamilton, L. (ed.) (1854). *Memoirs, Speeches and Writings of Robert Rantoul Jr*. Boston: John P. Jewett.

Haney, C., Sontag, L., and Costanzo, S. (1994). "Deciding to Take a Life." *Journal of Social Issues*, vol. 50, pp. 149–176.

Hansen, M. (June 1996). "From Death's Door." *American Bar Association Journal*, pp. 58–64.

Hanson, C. (October 31, 1995). "Few of Those Accused Get Dream Team." *Los Angeles Daily Journal*.

Hillman, H. (1993). "The Possible Pain Experienced during Execution by Different Methods." *Perception*, vol. 22, pp. 745–753.

Hook, D. D., and Kahn, L. (1989). *Death in the Balance*. Lexington, Mass.: D. C. Heath.

Hoppe, C. (March 8, 1992). "Executions Cost Texas Millions." *The Dallas Morning News*, p. A1.

Horwitz, E. L. (1973). *Capital Punishment, USA*. Philadelphia: J. B. Lippincott Co.

Hubler, S. (April 4, 1993). "A Slow Shift to the Fast Lane." *Los Angeles Times*. p. A1.

Johnson, R. (1981). *Condemned to Die: Life Under the Sentence of Death*. New York: Elsevier.

Johnson, R. (1990). *Death Work: A Study of the Modern Execution Process*. Pacific Grove, Cal.: Brooks/Cole.

Jurek v. Texas (1976). 428 U.S. 262.

Kane, K. (1986). "Forgotten Families of Death Row." *The Defender*, pp. 33–35.

Kant, I. (1797). *The Metaphysical Elements of Justice*. Indianapolis: Bobbs-Merrill (1965).

Kaplan, J. (1983). "The problem of Capital Punishment." *University of Illinois Law Review*, 88, pp. 555–577.

King, D. R. (1979). "The Brutalization Effect." *Social Forces*, vol. 57, pp. 683–687.

Klein, L. R., Forst, B. E., and Filatov, V. (1978). "The Deterrent Effect of Capital Punishment: An Assessment of the Estimates." In A. Blumstein, J. Cohen, and D. Nagin (eds.),

Deterrence and Incapacitation. Washington D.C.: National Academy of Sciences.

Koestler, A. (1957). *Reflections on Hanging.* New York: Macmillan.

Kolarik, G. (January 1996). "DNA, Changed Testimony, Gain Acquittal." *American Bar Association Journal,* pp. 34–35.

Laurence, J. (1931). *A History of Capital Punishment.* London: Sampson, Low, Marston & Company.

Lempert, R. O. (1983). "The Effect of Executions on Homicides: A New Look in an Old Light." *Crime and Delinquency,* vol. 29, pp. 88–115.

Locke, J. (1690). *Two Treatises of Government.* Cambridge University Press (1963).

Lockett v. Ohio (1978). 438 U.S. 586.

Los Angeles Times (January 8, 1995). "Faster Isn't Always Better." p. M4.

Luginbuhl, J., and Burkhead, M. (1994). "Sources of Bias and Arbitrariness in the Capital Trial." *Journal of Social Issues,* p. 103.

MacKenzie, D., and Goodstein, L. (1985). "Long-Term Incarceration Impacts and the Characteristics of Long-Term Offenders." *Criminal Justice and Behavior,* vol. 12, pp. 395–412.

Magagnini, S. (1988, March 28). "Closing Death Row Would Save State $90 Million a Year." *The Sacramento Bee,* p. 1.

Malinowski, B. (1954). *Magic, Science and Religion and Other Essays.* Garden City, New York: Doubleday.

Manning, C. (September 30, 1995). "Prisoner, Cleared of 1986 Slaying, Is Free." *Our World,* B1.

Marquart, J. W., Ekland-Olson, S., and Sorensen, J. R. (1994). *The Rope, the Chair, and the Needle: Capital Punishment in Texas, 1923–1990*. Austin: University of Texas.

Mayer-Schonberger, V. (1990). "Crossing the River of No Return: International Restrictions on the Death Penalty and the Execution of Charles Coleman." *Oklahoma Law Review*, vol. 43, pp. 670–692.

McCleskey v. Kemp (1987). 481 U.S. 279.

McGautha v. California (1971). 402 U.S. 183.

Mello, M. (1988). "Facing Death Alone: The Post-Conviction Attorney Crisis on Death Row." *The American University Law Review*, 37, pp. 513–607.

Melton, G. (1989). *Capital Punishment: Official Statements from Religious Bodies and Ecumenical Organizations*. Detroit: Gale Research Inc.

Millman, M. (ed.). (1986). *California Death Penalty Manual*. Los Angeles: California Association for Criminal Justice.

Moore, David W. (September 1994). "Majority Advocate Death Penalty for Teenage Killers." *The Gallup Poll Monthly*, pp. 2–6.

Moran, R., and Ellis, J. (June 14, 1989). "Death Penalty: Luxury Item." *New York Newsday*, p. 60.

Morganthau, T. (August 7, 1995). "Condemned to Life." *Newsweek*, pp. 19–23.

Nakell, B. (1982). "The Cost of the Death Penalty." In H. Bedau, *The Death Penalty in America*, pp. 241–246.

Nathanson, S. (1987). *An Eye for an Eye?* Totowa, New Jersey: Roman and Littlefield.

Newsweek. (July 28, 1995). "Killing Me Cruelly?"

Newton, J., and Frammolino, R. (September 10, 1994). "Prosecution Won't Seek Death Penalty Against Simpson." *Los Angeles Times*, p. A1.

Page, B. I., and Shapiro, R. Y. (1992). *The Rational Public.* Chicago University Press.

Paley, W. (1790). *Commentaries on the Laws of England*, vol. 4. Worcester, Mass.: Thomas.

Payne v. Tennessee (1991). 111 S.Ct. 2597.

Payton, R. (March 6, 1987). "How Parents of Slain Children Cope." *Oakland Tribune*, p. C7.

Paternoster, R. (1991). *Capital Punishment in America.* New York: Lexington Books.

Paternoster, R., and Kazyaka, A. M. (1988). "The Administration of the Death Penalty in South Carolina: Experiences Over the First Few Years." *South Carolina Law Review*, vol. 39, pp. 245–414.

People v. Kimble (1988). 488 U.S. 871.

Peterson, R. D., and Bailey, W. C. (1988). "Murder and Capital Punishment in the Evolving Context of the Post-Furman Era." *Social Forces*, vol. 66, pp. 774–807.

Pierce, G. L., and Radelet, M. L. (1991). "The Role and Consequences of the Death Penalty in American Politics." *New York University of Law and Social Change*, vol. 18, pp. 711–727.

Pope John Paul II (1995). *The Gospel of Life: On the Value and Inviolability of Human Life.* Washington, D.C.: United States Catholic Conference.

Press, A. (May 6, 1996). "The Great Writ Hit." *Newsweek*.

Profitt v. Florida (1976). 428 U.S. 242.

Radelet, M. L. (1989). "Executions of Whites for Crimes Against Blacks: Exceptions to the Rule?" *The Sociological Quarterly*, 30, pp. 529–541.

Radelet, M. L., and Bedau, H. A. (1988). "Fallibility and Finality: Type II Errors and Capital Punishment." In K. C. Haas and J. A. Inciardi (eds.), *Challenging Capital Punishment* (pp. 91–112). Newbury Park, Cal.: Sage.

Radelet, M. L., Bedau, H. A., Putnam, C. E. (1992). *In Spite of Innocence: Erroneous Convictions in Capital Cases*. Boston: Northeastern University Press.

Radelet, M. L., and Vandiver, M. (1983). "The Florida Supreme Court and Death Penalty Appeals." *Journal of Criminal Law and Criminology*, 74, pp. 913–926.

Reiman, J. (1988). "The Justice of the Death Penalty in an Unjust World." In K. C. Haas and J. A. Inciardi (eds.), *Challenging Capital Punishment* (pp. 29–48). Newbury Park, Cal.: Sage.

Reske, H. J. (November 1995). "The Politics of Death." *ABA Journal*, p. 20.

Robinson, R. J. (1993). "What Does 'Unwilling' to Impose the Death Penalty Mean Anyway?" *Law and Human Behavior*, 17, pp. 471–477.

Rohde, S. F. (Summer 1993). "Executing the Innocent." *The Sentry*, p. 3.

Rosenberg, H. (August 25, 1993). "Murderer Goes Out in a Blaze of Glory." *Los Angeles Times*.

Royal Commission Report on Capital Punishment (1953). London: Her Majesty's Stationery Office.

Saffle v. Parks (1990). 110 S.Ct. 1257.

Sahagun, L. (January 22, 1996). "Utah Is under Fire over Firing Squads." *Los Angeles Times*, p. A1.

San Francisco Chronicle (August 12, 1995). "Condemned Man's Stomach Pumped Before Execution." p. A4.

Sarat, A., and Vidmar, N. (1976). "The Public, the Death Penalty, and the Eighth Amendment." *Wisconsin Law Review*, 17, pp. 171 206.

Scheer, R. (February 19, 1995). "Equal Justice: $11.75 an Hour versus $1.5 Million." *Los Angeles Times*, p. M5.

Schneider, V., and Smykla, J. (1991). "A Summary Analysis of Executions in the United States, 1608–1987: The Espy File." In R. Bohm (ed.), *The Death Penalty in America: Current Perspectives* (pp. 1–19). Cincinnati, Ohio: Anderson.

Scott, G. R. (1950). *The History of Capital Punishment*. London: Torchstream Books.

Sellin, T. (1980). *The Penalty of Death*. Beverly Hills, Cal.: Sage Publications.

Sheppard, S. R. (1995). "In the Belly of the Death Penalty Beast." In *The Machinery of Death*. New York: Amnesty International USA.

Slovic, P., Fischoff, B., and Litchtenstein, K. (1982). "Facts versus Fears: Understanding Perceived Risk." In D. Kahneman, P. Slovic, and A. Tversky (eds.), *Judgment under Uncertainty: Heuristics and Biases*.

Smolowe, J. (April 29, 1991). "Race and the Death Penalty." *Time*.

Sorenson, J. R., and Marquart, J. W. (1989). "Working the Dead." In M. L. Radelet (ed.), *Facing the Death Penalty* (pp. 169–177). Philadelphia: Temple University Press.

Spangenberg, R. L., and Walsh, E. R. (1989). "Capital Punishment or Life Imprisonment? Some Cost Considerations." *Loyola of Los Angeles Law Review*, 23, pp. 45–58.

Tabak, R. J., and Lane, M. (1989). "The Execution of Justice: A Cost and Lack-of-Benefit Analysis of the Death Penalty." *Loyola of Los Angeles Law Review*, vol. 23 (2), pp. 59–146.

Thomas, C. W. (1977). "Eighth Amendment Challenges to the Death Penalty: The Relevance of Informed Public Opinion." *Vanderbilt Law Review*, vol. 30, pp. 1,005–1,030.

Thompson v. Oklahoma (1988) 487 U.S. 815.

Trombley, S. (1992). *The Execution Protocol: Inside America's Capital Punishment Industry*. New York: Crown Publishers.

Uelmen, G. F. (1996). *Lessons from the Trial: The People v. O. J. Simpson*. Kansas City: Andrews and McMeel.

Van den Haag, E., and Conrad, J. (1983). *The Death Penalty: A Debate*. New York: Plenum.

Vandiver, M. (1989). "Coping with Death." In M. L. Radelet (ed.), *Facing the Death Penalty*. Philadelphia: Temple University Press.

Von Drehle, D. (1995). *Among the Lowest of the Dead*. New York: Times Books.

Von Drehle, D. (1988, July 10). "Bottom Line: Life in Prison One-Sixth as Expensive." *The Miami Herald*, p. 12A.

Wainwright v. Witt (1985). 105 S. Ct. 844.

Wallace, A. (April 22, 1992). "Relatives of Two Victims Weigh Emotional Toll." *Los Angeles Times*.

Weinstein, H., and Abrahamson, A. (July 10, 1994). "Death Penalty Unlikely for Simpson, Experts Say." *Los Angeles Times*, p. A1.

Weisberg, R. (1984). "Deregulating Death." In P. Kurland, G. Casper, and D. Hutchinson (eds.), *The Supreme Court Review*, 1983 (pp. 305–395). University of Chicago Press.

Weizman, S. G., and Kamm, P. (1985). *About Mourning*. New York: Human Sciences Press.

Witherspoon v. Illinois (1968). 391 U.S. 510.

Wolfgang, M., and Riedel, M. (1973). "Race, Judicial Discretion, and the Death Penalty." *Annals of the American Academy of Political and Social Science*, 407, pp. 119–133.

Woodson v. North Carolina (1976). 428 U.S. 280.

Woodward, B., and Armstrong, S. (1979). *The Brethren: Inside the Supreme Court*. New York: Avon.

Wright, J. H. (1990). "Life without Parole: An Alternative to Death or Not Much of a Life at All?" *Vanderbilt Law Review*, vol. 43, pp. 529–568.

Zimring, F. E., and Hawkins, G. (1986). *Capital Punishment and the American Agenda*. Cambridge University Press.

Index